THE

STANDARD MANUAL

FOR

BAPTIST CHURCHES

THE

STANDARD MANUAL

FOR

BAPTIST CHURCHES.

BY

EDWARD T. HISCOX, D.D.

GYAN

Published by

GYAN

Gyan Publishing House
5, Ansari Road
Daryaganj, New Delhi-110002
Phone: 011-47034999, 9811692060
E-mail: books@gyanbooks.com

Distribution Network
gyanbooks.com
India, USA, Canada, UK, Australia

ISBN: 978-93-6208-540-5 (PB)
First Published, 1890

2nd Impression 2024

Printed at: Gyan Press, Delhi.

THE STANDARD MANUAL FOR BAPTIST CHURCHES
Author: EDWARD T. HISCOX

THE

STANDARD MANUAL

FOR

BAPTIST CHURCHES.

BY

EDWARD T. HISCOX, D. D.,

Author of "The Baptist's Short Method," "Star Book for Ministers," "The Star Book Series," "Pastors' Manual," etc.

PHILADELPHIA:

AMERICAN BAPTIST PUBLICATION SOCIETY,

1420 Chestnut Street.

CONTENTS.

PREFACE.

It is now thirty years since the "Baptist Church Directory," prepared by the writer, was first published. That work was designed to be somewhat of a *consensus* of the opinions of those best able to judge in matters of Baptist Church polity and usage, especially as to what concerns administration and discipline. It might thus prove a help to both pastors and members, particularly in perplexing cases liable to arise. Thus it was hoped it might help to rectify the order and customs of our churches through our widely extended ranks. This hope has been realized. More than fifty thousand copies of that book have been circulated in this country. It has also been translated, more or less fully, into six or seven different languages by our missionaries, for use in our missions and foreign fields.

But many of the churches desired a smaller and less expensive manual, which they could put into the hands of all their members. To meet this want, sixteen years ago, the writer prepared the little "Star Book on Baptist Church Polity," which many churches have adopted, furnishing their members and candidates for membership with them freely. This has had a circulation of over thirty thousand copies; and both this and the "Directory" are in as great demand as at any previous time.

It is something more than twenty years since the "Baptist Short Method," by the same author was published. The purpose of this manual was to give a concise view of those distinctive features which mark the difference between Baptists and other denominations, especially as to the ordinances and church order; and also to furnish the proofs by which our position in these respects is justified. About ten thousand copies of this book have found their way into circulation.

The preparation of the present manual was undertaken at the request, and by an arrangement with the pastor, R. S. MacArthur, D. D., on behalf of the Calvary

Baptist Church, New York City, for the special use of that church. Something was desired smaller than the "Directory," and more full than the "Star Book," embracing certain features of the "Short Method." When completed, it was thought to be, on the whole, so much superior to anything ever before prepared, as a manual for general use in Baptist churches, that by mutual consent, it was decided to have it published for general circulation, rather than confine it to the use of a single church.

To both ministers and members, such a manual, it is hoped, will prove a valuable helper in the interest of church order, and of denominational unity and prosperity. Especially for the younger members, so many thousands of whom are yearly admitted to the fellowship of the churches, with an unlimited franchise, while but imperfectly instructed as to either doctrines or order, it should prove a most valuable assistant. Concise and accurate in statement of facts, transparent in arrangement of matters, convenient in form, and cheap in cost, pastors will find it to their own advantage, as well as to that of their members, to see that their churches are liberally supplied with copies. The pastor of one of our very largest and most prosperous churches, for whose use its preparation was undertaken, shows his estimate of its value, and sets other pastors a wise and worthy example, by ordering in advance of publication, *one thousand copies* for his church.

May the divine blessing make this, as other works have been made, a means of furthering good order, spiritual vitality, and efficient service for Christ, in the churches for which it is designed.

Mount Vernon, N. Y.,
January 24, 1890. E. T. H.

STANDARD MANUAL

FOR

BAPTIST CHURCHES.

CHAPTER I.

A CHRISTIAN CHURCH.

THE word "church" is, in common language, used with large latitude of meaning. It is applied to a building used for Christian worship, to a congregation of Christian worshipers, to a religious establishment, to a given form of ecclesiastical order, to the aggregate of all Christian believers, and to a local company of Christian disciples associated in covenant for religious purposes. The latter is its common use in the New Testament.

The Greek word *ekklesia,* rendered "church" is derived from a word meaning "called out," and is used to indicate a company called out from a larger and more general assembly or concourse of people. In the free Greek cities, it designated a company of persons possessed of the rights of citizenship, and charged with certain important functions of administration in public affairs, summoned, or called out, from the common mass of the people. In the New Testament, the *ekklesia* is a company of persons called out and separated from the common multitude by a divine calling, chosen to be saints, invested with the privileges, and charged with the duties of citizenship in the kingdom of Christ.

A Christian church, therefore, according to the New Testament idea, is a company of persons divinely called and separated from the world, baptized on a profession of their faith in Christ, united in covenant for worship and Christian service, under the supreme authority of Christ, whose word is their only law and rule of life in all matters of religious faith and practice.

Some Christian denominations include all their congregations in one comprehensive society, or ecclesiastical system, under some central authority, which legislates for and controls the whole. This comprehensive society they call the church. Thus we speak of the Roman Catholic Church, the Episcopal Church, the Presbyterian Church —where the word "church" stands for the aggregate of all their local societies. With Baptists it is different. They speak of Baptist churches, but not of the Baptist Church, when the entire denomination is meant. The Baptist Church would mean some one local congregation of baptized believers.

Thus was it in apostolic times. There was "the church in Jerusalem," "the church of the Thessalonians," "the church of Babylon," "the church of the Laodiceans"; but "the churches of Macedonia," "the churches of Asia," "the churches of Judea." A church, therefore, is not a system of congregations confederated under a general government, but a single local congregation of Christian disciples asssociated in covenant and meeting together for worship. In this sense the word is commonly, almost uniformly, used in the New Testament.

Churches are divinely instituted to be "the light of the world" and "the salt or the earth." They are ordained for the glory of God, as "the ground and pillar of the truth," in the proclamation of his gospel and the establishment of his kingdom in the world. They are commissioned to preach the gospel to men, and to live the gospel before men, that Christ may be honored and sinners saved. They should, therefore, be constantly striving to realize the grand purpose of their existence and fulfill the mission of their high calling. That church which does the most to honor Christ and save man will be the most honored by him, and the most influential and prosperous in all that pertains to the true functions of a church. And since a church, as a body, is what its individual members are in their religious life and influence, therefore each member should strive to become in holy living what he desires the church to be.

NOTE 1.—A body of Christian disciples may fail to meet some of the requirements of the gospels, and still be a true church of Christ, providing it fulfills the fundamental conditions of a Scriptural faith and practice.

NOTE 2.—But when a body ceases to acknowledge and submit to Christ as its Supreme Ruler, and to receive his word as its supreme law, then it ceases to

be a true church, and is simply a religious society, though it may still accept some of his doctrines and practice some of his precepts.

NOTE 3.—A church is not a legislative, but an executive body. It cannot make laws, but only obey and administer those which Christ has given in the New Testament. He is the only Lawmaker in Zion.

NOTE 4.—But in matters pertaining to order and methods of administration, merely optional and discretionary, not involving fundamental principles, the church is to exercise its liberty, so long as it does not contravene Scriptural teaching or infringe the rights of its members.

NOTE 5.—And still further, while a church cannot become an authoritative expounder of either truth or duty, to bind the consciences even of its members, yet it does possess a judicial function for the interpretation and the enforcement of the laws of Christ for itself as a body, and, therefore, for its members, so far as their relation to the compact is concerned.

NOTE 6.—Each church owes courtesy and comity, fellowship and fraternity, to all others; but it owes subjection and allegiance to none, and is under authority to Christ alone.

NOTE 7.—In matters of business and in the exercise of its authority in administration, the will of the church is expressed by a majority vote of its members. But the nearer that majority approaches to unanimity, the more satisfactory and emphatic are its decisions.

NOTE 8.—Councils may be called, presbyteries convened, or committees of reference chosen for advice in cases of moment, but they are all *advisory* only, and in no case authoritative. There is no higher, and no other court of appeal in ecclesiastical affairs, than the individual church.

CHAPTER II.

CHURCH OFFICERS.[1]

The Scriptural officers of a church are *bishops* and *deacons.* Bishops are in the New Testament also called "presbyters," "elders," and "overseers." Their duties and services have mainly reference to the spiritual interests of the body, though they properly have the oversight of all its concerns. The deacons have principal charge of the temporalities of the church, so as to relieve the pastor in that department of labor. They are, however, to be counselors and helpers of the pastor in all departments of his work. The qualifications for both offices are set forth in the Epistles to Timothy and Titus.

NOTE 1.—Pastors and deacons, as teachers and leaders of the flock, cannot be selected for and imposed upon the churches by any external authority whatever, either civic or religious; but are elected

---

[1] This and several of the following sections are consistent with the "Star Book on Baptist Church Polity," on the same topics.

and chosen by the free suffrages of the members, without compulsion or restraint, from among themselves, or those who are to become identified with them in fellowship.

NOTE 2.—In the election of either a pastor or deacon, notice of such election should be given from the pulpit for at least two Sundays preceding the time for the same. The election should be by ballot, and at least *three-quarters* of the votes cast should be necessary for the election of a pastor, and *two-thirds* for the election of a deacon. Such election should be preceded by prayer for divine direction, and conducted without partisan devices or personal strife.

NOTE 3.—Both pastors and deacons are properly elected for unlimited terms of service, the relation to continue so long as there shall be mutual satisfaction. Such a course tends less to depreciate and make servile the officers and their duties in the estimation of the people, and of those who bear them, than a limited and specified time, though deacons are sometimes, and perhaps properly, chosen for a limited term of service, subject to re-election, at the option of the church.

NOTE 4.—The church is to fix on the amount of salary necessary to a generous support of the pastor, and hold itself obligated by every consideration of Christian honor for the prompt and regular payment of the same. To fail in this is as dishonorable to the church as it is unjust and vexatious to the pastor.

NOTE 5.—The call to a pastor issues from the *church* as a body, which also designates the amount of salary to be paid. It is in some sections usual, though not essential, to have subsequently a meeting of the entire congregation or society to approve or confirm the call. In some States it is neccessary for the trustees, as the legal representatives of the corporation, to confirm the action officially, so far as the salary is concerned, before it can become legal.

NOTE 6.—The number of deacons is optional with the church. It is usually from *three* to *seven*. Let it be so many as the church needs and can find suitable candidates for the supply. But they should never be elected simply to fill the office, and never unless there be persons whose fitness for the office is generally conceded.

NOTE 7.—The relations between pastor and the church may be dissolved at the option of either, by giving *three months* notice; or otherwise, by mutual consent. Between the deacons and the church, the relations may be dissolved at the option of either without previous notice.

NOTE 8.—A church *clerk* is elected annually, at a business meeting, by a majority vote. It is an office of convenience, for keeping the minutes and preserving the records of the body. Also *trustees* are elected by the church, or if the law so requires, by a *society*. Their duties are the care of the property and the management of finances. But these are not considered Scriptural church officers; deacons might properly discharge all the functions of these offices.[1]

NOTE 9.—The offices of trust and service in a

[1] In some States the laws do not recognize the church, that being a spiritual body, but incorporate a *society*, as it is called, consisting of all persons of full age who attend and support the worship. This society has charge of the financial affairs of the church, hold and keep in repair its property, and conduct its secular concerns. It elects a specified number of *trustees*, as provided for by law, who are the legal representatives of the corporation. The members of the society, and the trustees elected, may or may not be members of the church. This whole society arrangement is a relict of the old New England parish system of the standing order, and is inconsistent with the freedom of church action, and antagonistic to Baptist Church independence. It is anti-Baptistic and anti-Scriptural. A church should be allowed to manage its own affairs, both temporal and spiritual: and should be protected by law in doing so. The society system has been abrogated in most of the States.

church should be as widely distributed among the members as possible, consistently with the welfare of the body. This rule should seldom be disregarded. No one man should hold more than one office at the same time, unless the interests of the body absolutely demand it. If offices are honors, they should be widely dispensed; if they are burdens, they certainly should be. For the same man to hold two or three offices is as unjust to him as it is to his brethren.

NOTE 10.—A church cannot unite in any corporate capacity with other organizations for religious, benevolent, moral reform, or other purposes; but it may coöperate with these for any good object, and give to such societies its moral support, sympathy, and pecuniary aid.

NOTE 11.—But members of churches can, as individuals, unite with outside organizations, for any purpose, not inconsistent with their profession as Christians, and not injurious to their church relations and duties.

NOTE 12.—Churches cannot alienate their responsibilities, nor delegate their authority to any man, or to any body of men, to act officially for them. But they can appoint persons to bear messages, and to perform services for them, under instruction, and to report their action to the body.

CHAPTER III.

CHURCH ORDINANCES.

CHRISTIAN ordinances, in the largest sense, are any institutions, or regulations of divine appointment, established as means of grace for the good of men, or as acts of worship for the honor of God. In that sense, not only are baptism and the Lord's Supper ordinances, but preaching, prayer, hearing the word, fasting, and thanksgiving are also ordinances, since all are of divine appointment. But, in a narrower sense, it is common to say that *baptism* and the *Lord's Supper* are the only ordinances appointed by Christ to be observed by his churches. These are the only emblematic and commemorative rites enjoined upon his disciples, by which they are to be distinguished, and he is to be honored. They are the two symbols and witnesses of the New Covenant, the two monuments of the New Dispensation.

Baptism is the immersion, or dipping, of a candidate in water, on a profession of his faith in Christ and on evidence of regeneration; the baptism to be ministered in, or into the name of the Father, the Son, and Holy Spirit. It represents the burial and resurrection of Christ, and in a figure declares the candidate's death to sin and the world, and his rising to a new life. It also proclaims the washing of regeneration, and professes the candidate's hope of a resurrection from the dead, through him into the likeness of whose death he is buried in baptism.

The Lord's Supper is a provision of bread and wine, used to represent the body and the blood of Christ, partaken of by members of the church assembled for that purpose; in which service they commemorate the love of Christ exhibited in his death for them, and profess their faith and participation in the merits of his sacrifice as the only ground of their hope of eternal life.

NOTE 1.—No person can rightfully or properly become a church member except he be first baptized, as the distinguishing mark and profession of his discipleship.

NOTE 2.—The Supper is a church ordinance, and therefore is the privilege of church members only.

Therefore, also, since baptism precedes church membership, it must precede and be pre-requisite to the Lord's Supper.

NOTE 3.—Since the Supper is distinctively a church ordinance, it is to be observed by churches only, and not by individuals; neither in private places, nor in sick rooms, nor on social occasions, and not by companies of disciples other than churches. But a church may by appointment, and in its official capacity, meet in a private house, a sick room, or wherever it may elect, and there observe the Supper.

NOTE 4.—Both ordinances are ordinarily and properly administered by ordained and accredited ministers; but both would be equally valid if administered by unordained persons, should occasion require and the church so direct. As to the qualifications of the administrator, the New Testament is silent, except that he should be a disciple.

NOTE 5.—As to the time, place, and frequency of the ordinances, no Scriptural directions are given. These are left optional with the churches. They are usually observed on Sundays, but not necessarily. As to the Supper, our churches have very generally come to observe it on the first Sunday of each month.

NOTE 6.—The participation of the elements in the Supper should be done according to the special direction of Christ, the Head of the body. "This do in remembrance of *me*." It is not, therefore, a test or token of Christian fellowship, except incidentally. All thought and sympathy in the service should be centered on him who is "the living bread," and not fixed on others.

NOTE 7.—The ordinances are not *sacraments*, as taught by some, conveying effectual grace to the soul and imparting spiritual life. But as divinely appointed means of grace, their importance must not be undervalued. They cannot be neglected without suffering serious harm and incurring the gravest responsibility.

NOTE 8.—Baptism is not essential to salvation, for our churches utterly repudiate the dogma of "baptismal regeneration"; but it is essential to obedience, since Christ has commanded it. It is also essential to a public confession of Christ before the world, and to membership in the church which is his body. And no true lover of his Lord will refuse these acts of obedience and tokens of affection.

CHAPTER IV.

CHURCH MEMBERSHIP.

IT is most likely that in the Apostolic age when there was but "one Lord, one faith, and one baptism," and no differing denominations existed, the baptism of a convert by that very act, constituted him a member of the church, and at once endowed him with all the rights and privileges of full membership. In that sense, "baptism was the door into the church." Now, it is different; and while the churches are desirous of receiving members, they are wary and cautious that they do not receive unworthy persons. The churches therefore have candidates come before them, make their statement, give their "experience," and then their reception is decided by a vote of the members. And while they cannot become members without baptism, yet it is the vote of the body which admits them to its fellowship on receiving baptism.

There are *three classes* of candidates, and modes of reception to membership.

1. *By baptism.*—The church having listened to the religious experience of the candidate, and being satisfied with the same, and with his Christian deportment, votes to receive him to its fellowship, "on being baptized."

2. *By letter.*—The candidate presents a letter of dismission and recommendation from some other Baptist church with which he has been connected, for the purpose of transferring his membership to this. The church, being satisfied, votes to receive him into fellowship.

3. *By experience.*—Persons having been baptized, but for some reason being without membership in any church, wish to be received. They, giving satisfactory evidence of Christian character, and substantial agreement in matters of faith and practice, are received by vote, as in other cases.

NOTE 1.—Persons cannot be received to membership on the credit of letters from other denominations. Such letters are, however, accepted, as certificates of Christian character, and of church standing.

NOTE 2.—While the churches do not require candidates to sign any creed, confession, or articles of faith, yet they do expect a substantial agreement in matters of faith and practice on their part as essential both to the comfort of the individual, and the harmony of the body.

NOTE 3.—Should any member object to the reception of a candidate, such reception should be deferred, in order to consider the reasons for the objection. Objections judged groundless or unreasonable should not prevent the reception of a suitable candidate; yet no one should be received except by a unanimous or nearly unanimous vote.

NOTE 4. It is customary for candidates, after their experience or letters have been presented, to retire while the church deliberates and acts upon their case.

NOTE 5.—Any member in good standing, is entitled, at any time, to a letter of dismission, in the usual form, with which to unite with another church of the same faith and order.

NOTE 6.—Letters are usually made valid for *six months* only, during which time they must be used, if used at all. But if held longer, they may be renewed by the church, if satisfactory reasons are given for their non-use.

NOTE 7.—Each one receiving a letter is still a member of the church, and under its watchcare and discipline, until his letter is actually received by another church.

NOTE 8.—Letters cannot be given to members for the purpose of uniting with churches with which we are not in fellowship. But any member is entitled, at any time, to receive a certificate of standing, and Christian character.

NOTE 9.—No member can *withdraw* from the church, or have his name *dropped*, or at his own request be *excluded* from the fellowship of the body without due process of discipline.

NOTE 10.—Nor can a member have a letter voted

and forced upon him without his wish and consent. Such would be a virtual expulsion from the body. If worthy to receive a letter, he cannot be forced out of the church against his will.

NOTE 11.—Members living remote from the church are expected to unite with some Baptist church near their residence; or give satisfactory reasons for not doing so. When they cannot so unite, they are expected to report themselves to the church at least *once each year*, and contribute to its support, till they cease to be members.

NOTE 12.—Letters of dismission may be revoked, at any time before being used, if, in the judgment of the church, there be sufficient cause for such action.

NOTE 13.—Church fellowship will be withdrawn from members who unite with other denominations; because, however excellent their character, or sincere their intentions, they have broken covenant with the church, and by such act have placed themselves beyond the limits of its fellowship.

NOTE 14.—Persons excluded from other churches are not to be received to membership, except after the most careful investigation of all the facts in the case, and not unless it be manifest that the exclusion was unjustifiable, and that the church excluding persistently refuses to do justice to the excluded member.

NOTE 15.—A letter is usually asked for and addressed to a particular church. This is proper, but not always necessary. It may in certain cases be asked for, and given "to any church of the same faith and order." Or if directed to one, it may be presented to, and received by another.

NOTE 16.—It is expected that all pecuniary liability to the church will be canceled, and all personal difficulties in the church will be settled by a member, should such exist, before he shall receive a letter of dismission.

NOTE 17.—Each member, without exception, is expected to fill his place in the church, by attendance on its appointments, as Providence may allow, and also to contribute of his means for the pecuniary support of the body, according to his ability. If in either of these respects he fails, and refuses, he becomes a covenant-breaker, and is subject to the discipline of the body.

NOTE 18.—Persons excluded from the church may be again received to its fellowship on satisfactory evidence of fitness. This is called reception by *restoration*, and is usually so entered on the records, and in associational reports.

NOTE 19.—It is neither a Christian nor an honorable course for a church to grant an unworthy member a valid letter, and send him to another church as one in good and regular standing, in order to be rid of a disturber of the peace, or to avoid the trouble of a course of discipline.

NOTE 20.—No church is *obliged* to receive a person to membership, simply because he brings a valid letter from another church. Each church is to be sole judge of the qualifications of persons to be received to its fellowship.

CHAPTER V.

CHURCH DISCIPLINE.

CHURCH members are supposed to be regenerate persons bearing the image and cherishing the spirit of Christ, in whom the peace of God rules, and who walk and work in "the unity of the Spirit, and the bond of peace." But unhappily, even the saints are sanctified only in part, and troubles sometimes arise among brethren. The evil passions of even good men may triumph over piety, and partisan strife may destroy the peace and the prosperity of the body of Christ. All this should, if possible, be avoided. Corrective discipline seeks to heal offenses; but it is better to *prevent* them, than to *heal* them. It is, however, better to heal and remove, than to endure them.

Now these offenses and occasions of dissension in the churches arise from various causes, and are largely preventable. Most frequently they come by the following means:

1. Because of the too suspicious and sensitive disposition of some who imagine themselves wronged, neglected, or in some way injured; the matter being chiefly imaginary, and without any real foundation in fact.

2. Because the pastor, deacons, and influential members do not carefully and constantly enough watch the beginnings of strife, and rectify the evil before it becomes serious.

3. Because evil-doers by delay become more persistent in evil, while others are drawn into the strife, and contentious parties insensibly are formed, which tend to divide the church into hostile factions.

4. Because that when the difficulty becomes chronic and deep-seated, the church is likely to undertake the discipline with judicial severity, and not in the spirit of meekness, in which the spiritual should restore the erring.

5. Because that a case of discipline undertaken under excitement is almost certain to be wrongly conducted. Even if the result reached be just and right, the method by

which it is reached is likely to be unwise, unjust, and oppressive to individuals, possibly producing more serious and more lasting evils than it has removed.

Offenses calling for discipline are usually considered as of *two* classes; *private* or personal, and *public* or general. These terms do not very accurately express the nature of the offenses, but they are in common use, and capable of being understood. In the administration of *corrective discipline*, the following rules and principles constitute a correct and Scriptural course of proceeding.

PRIVATE OFFENSES.

Private offenses pertain to personal difficulties between individuals, having no direct reference to the church as a body, and not involving the Christian profession at large. In such cases, the course prescribed by our Saviour (Matt. 18 : 15–17) is to be strictly followed, without question or deviation.

1. *First step.*—The member who considers himself injured must go to the offender, tell him his grief, and between themselves alone, if possible, adjust and settle the difficulty. "If thy brother shall trespass against thee, go and tell him his

fault, between thee and him alone." This must be done, not to charge, upbraid, or condemn the offender, but to win him. "If he shall hear thee, thou hast gained thy brother."

2. *Second step.*—If this shall fail, then the offended member must take one or two of the brethren with him as witnesses, seek an interview with the offender, and, if possible, by their united wisdom and piety, remove the offense and harmonize the difficulty. "But if he will not hear thee, then take with thee one or two more, that in the mouth of two or three witnesses, every word may be established."

3. *Third step.*—If this step should prove unavailing, then the offended member must tell the whole matter to the *church,* and leave it in their hands to be disposed of, as to them may seem wisest and best. "And if he shall neglect to hear them, tell it to the church." He has done his duty and must abide by the decision of the body which assumes this responsibility.

4. *The result.*—If this course of kindly Christian labor proves finally ineffectual, and the offender shows himself incorrigible, excision must follow. He must be cut off

from fellowship in the church whose covenant he has broken, and whose authority he disregards. "And if he neglect to hear the church, let him be unto thee as an heathen man, and a publican." However painful the act, the church must be faithful to its duty, and to its God.

NOTE 1.—While this divine rule makes it obligatory on the offended member to go to the offender and seek a reconciliation, yet much more is it obligatory on the offender who knows that a brother is grieved with him, to seek such an one, and try to remove the difficulty.

NOTE 2.—The matter is not to be made public until these three steps have been fully taken, and have failed; and then to be made public only by telling the church, and no others.

NOTE 3.—When the case comes before the church, it must not be neglected, nor dropped, but judiciously pursued until the difficulty be adjusted, the offense removed, or else the offender be disfellowshipped, and put away.

PUBLIC OFFENSES.

Public offenses are not against any one person more than another, but are such as are supposed to be a dishonor to the church of which the offender is a member, and a reproach to the Christian profession. They constitute a violation of the code of Christian morals, if not of our common worldly morals.

The more common causes of this class of offenses are the following: False doctrine (Gal. 1 : 9; 2 John 10), disregard of authority (Matt. 18 : 17; 1 Thess. 5 : 14), contention and strife (Rom. 16 : 17), immoral conduct (1 Cor. 5 : 11), disorderly walk (2 Thess. 3 : 6, 9), covetous spirit (Eph. 5 : 5; 1 Cor. 5 : 11), arrogant conduct (3 John 9), going to law (1 Cor. 6 : 6).

The following constitutes a proper and Scriptural course of treatment for such cases:

1. The first member who has knowledge of the offense should, as in the case of private offenses, seek the offender, ascertain the facts, and attempt to reconcile or remove the difficulty. Not till he has done this should he make it public, or bring it before the church.

2. But if no one will, or can, pursue this course of personal effort, or if such a course proves unsuccessful, then any member having knowledge of the facts should confer with the pastor and deacons as to the best course to be pursued.

3. The pastor and deacons should, by the best method they are capable of devising, labor to adjust the matter without bringing

it into the church, or otherwise making it public.

4. But if their efforts fail, or if the case be already public, and a reproach and scandal to religion, then they should bring it to the church, and it should direct a proper course of discipline.

5. The church, thus having the case before it, should either appoint a committee to visit the offender, or cite him before the body to answer the charge. He should be allowed to hear the evidence against him, know the witnesses, and be permitted to answer for himself.

6. If the accused disproves the charges, or if he confesses the wrong, makes suitable acknowledgment, and, so far as possible, reparation, with promise of amendment, in all ordinary cases, this should be deemed satisfactory, and the case be dismissed.

7. But if, after patient, deliberate, and prayerful labor, all efforts fail to reclaim the offender, then, however painful the necessity, the church must withdraw its fellowship from him, and put him away from them.

8. If the case be one of flagrant immorality, by which the reputation of the body

is compromised and the Christian name scandalized, on being proven or confessed, the hand of fellowship may be at once withdrawn from the offender, notwithstanding any confessions and promises of amendment; but not without a trial.

The church's good name and the honor of religion demand this testimony against evil. He may be subsequently restored, if suitably penitent.

NOTE. 1.—All discipline should be conducted in the spirit of Christian meekness and love, with a desire to remove offenses and win offenders. It must also be done under a deep sense of responsibility to maintain the honor of Christ's name, the purity of his church, and the integrity of his truth.

NOTE 2.—If any member shall persist in bringing a private grievance before the church, or otherwise make it public, before he has pursued the course prescribed in the eighteenth chapter of Matthew, he becomes himself an offender, and subject to the discipline of the body.

NOTE 3.—When private difficulties exist among members, which they cannot, or will not settle, the church should consider them as public offenses, and as such dispose of them, rather than suffer the perpetual injury which they inflict.

NOTE 4.—When a member refers to the church any private difficulty, which he has been unable to settle, he must submit it wholly to the disposition of the body, and abide by its decision. If he attempts to revive and prosecute it beyond the decision of the church, he becomes an offender, and subject to discipline.

NOTE 5.—Any member tried by the church has the right to receive copies of all charges against him, the names of his accusers and the witnesses, both of whom he shall have the privilege of meeting face to face, hearing their statements, bringing witnesses on his side, and answering for himself before the body.

NOTE 6.—Every member, on trial or excluded, shall have furnished, at his request, authentic copies of all proceedings had by the church in his case, officially certified.

NOTE 7.—No member under discipline can have the right to bring any person, not a member, before the church as his advocate, except by consent of the body.

NOTE 8.—In every case of exclusion, the charges against the member, and the reasons for his exclusion, should be accurately entered on the records of the church.

NOTE 9.—If at any time it shall become apparent, or seem probable to the church that it has for any reason dealt unjustly with a member, or excluded him without sufficient cause, it should at once, and without request, by concession and restoration, so far as possible, repair the injury it has done him.

NOTE 10.—The church should hold itself bound to restore to its fellowship an excluded member whenever he gives satisfactory evidence of repentance and reformation consistent with godliness.

NOTE 11.—The church will exercise its legitimate authority, and vindicate its honor and rectitude in the administration of discipline, even though the member should regard such discipline as unjust or oppressive.

NOTE 12.—Nothing can be considered a just and reasonable cause for discipline, except what is forbidden by the letter or the spirit of Scripture. And nothing can be considered a sufficient cause for disfellowship and exclusion, except what is clearly contrary to Scripture, and what would have prevented the reception of the person into the church, had it been known to exist at the time of his reception.

CHAPTER VI.

CASES OF APPEAL.

CASES of difficulty and discipline do sometimes occur, so aggravated in their nature or so complicated in their treatment that it is found impossible to make a satisfactory settlement by ordinary methods; especially so if discipline has ended in exclusion. The excluded member will be almost sure to think he has been dealt with unjustly, and will wish for some redress; and if the case has been of long standing and much complicated, he will be equally sure to have others sympathize with him and condemn the action of the church. Now, although the *presumption* is that the church has done right, and is justified in its action, the *possibility* is that the church has done wrong, and is censurable for its action.

What can be done in such a case?

NOTE 1.—On the New Testament theory of church government, the action of the individual local church is final. There is no power, either civil or ecclesiastical, that can reverse its decision or punish it for wrongdoing. It may make mistakes, but no human tribunal has authority to compel it to confess or correct them.

NOTE 2.—Councils, if appealed to for redress, have *no authority;* they are simply, always, and everywhere *advisory*—that, and nothing more. They can express an opinion, and give advice; but they have no authority to issue decrees, and would have no power to enforce them if they should.[1]

NOTE 3.—Any person who believes himself wronged by church action has the inalienable right to appeal to the church for a new hearing, and, failing in this, to ask the counsel and advice of brethren, should he see fit to do so.

Now observe—If an excluded member believes himself unjustly dealt by, and wishes redress, the following is the proper course for him to pursue:

1. Apply to the church which excluded, and ask a re-hearing. State to them the grounds of his complaint and the evidence on which he thinks he can satisfy them, if a fair opportunity for being heard be given him.

2. If they refuse him a re-hearing, let him appeal to them to unite with him in calling a *mutual council*, before which the

---

[1] For a more comprehensive discussion of *councils*—what they can, and what they cannot do, how to call, and how to use them—see the "Star Book on Baptist Councils."

whole case shall be placed, all parties to abide by its decision.

3. If a mutual council be declined by the church, he would be fully justified, should he feel so inclined, in calling an *ex parte* council, before which he should place the facts and seek its advice.

4. Or, instead of calling an *ex parte* council, he could apply to some other church to be received to its fellowship, on the ground that he had been unjustly excluded. Should he be received to another church, that would give him church standing and fellowship again, and vindicate him so far as any ecclesiastical action could vindicate him.

5. If all these resorts fail, there is nothing left but for him to wait patiently and bear the burden of his wrong until Providence opens the way for his deliverance. He may, after all, conclude that he himself was more in fault than he at first supposed, and the church less so.

Note 4.—An *ex parte* council should not be called in such a case of difficulty until all efforts have failed to secure a *mutual* council; as such a council, if called, would probably do nothing more than advise a mutual council and adjourn.

Note 5.—Any church can well afford to grant a re-hearing to an excluded member. It would be in

the interest of peace, justice, and reconciliation. If the church be right, it can afford to be generous.

NOTE 6.—Any church has the right to receive a member excluded from another church, since each church is sole judge of the qualification of persons received to its fellowship. But any church so appealed to would use great caution, and, with due regard to its own peace and purity, ascertain all the facts in the case before taking such action.

NOTE 7.—If a mutual council be called, one-half the messengers and members are to be chosen by the church and one-half by the aggrieved party; but the *letters missive* calling the council are to be sent out by and in the name of the church, and not of the aggrieved party. But these facts, as to the mutual call, are to be stated in the letters.

NOTE 8.—A church excluding a member has no just cause of complaint against another church for receiving such an excluded member, since the one church is just as independent to receive one whom it judges worthy of fellowship, as the other is to exclude one whom it judged unworthy of fellowship.

CHAPTER VII.

CHURCH BUSINESS.

THE business meetings of a church should be conducted as much as possible in the spirit of devotion, and under a sense of the propriety and sanctity which attaches to all the interests of the kingdom of Christ. Meetings for business should not be needlessly multiplied, nor should they be unwisely neglected. It may not be wise to insist too rigidly on the observance of parliamentary rules, yet it is still worse to drift into a loose unbusinesslike way, which wastes time, accomplishes little, and does wrongly much that is done.

ORDER OF BUSINESS.

1. The meetings to be opened with reading the Scriptures, singing, and prayer.
2. The reading, correction, and approval of the minutes of the preceding meeting.
3. Unfinished business, or such as the

minutes present, including reports of committee taken in order.

4. New business will next be taken up. Any member may call up new business. But important matters should not be presented, except on previous consultation with the pastor and deacons.

NOTE 1.—The pastor is, by virtue of his office, moderator of all church business meetings. If he be not present, or do not wish to serve, any one may be elected to take the place.

NOTE 2.—All business meetings, both regular and special, should be announced from the pulpit one Sunday, at least, before they are held.

NOTE 3.—Special meetings for business may be called at any time, by consent of the pastor and deacons, or by such other methods as the church itself may direct.

NOTE 4.—Though a majority usually decides questions, yet in all matters of special importance a unanimous, or nearly unanimous, vote should be secured.

NOTE 5.—Members may be received, and letters of dismission granted, either at the business church meeting, the covenant meeting, or the regular weekly prayer meeting, the church so directing. Some fixed method should be observed.

NOTE 6.—Candidates for admission to membership will be expected to retire from the meeting when action is taken on their reception.

NOTE 7.—No persons, except members, will be present during the transaction of church business. If present, they may be asked to retire.

NOTE 8.—Although the church should endeavor to do nothing which its members will be ashamed or afraid to have known by others, yet every member is bound, by the honor of a Christian, not to publish abroad, nor disclose to those without, the private affairs and business transactions of the body.

RULES OF ORDER.

The following constitute the generally accepted rules of order for churches and other deliberative bodies in business proceedings:

Motions.

1. All business shall be presented by a *motion*, made by one member, and seconded by another, and presented in writing by the mover. if so required.

2. No discussion can properly be had until the motion is made, seconded, and stated by the chairman.

3. A motion cannot be withdrawn after it has been discussed, except by the unanimous consent of the body.

4. A motion having been discussed, must be put to vote, unless withdrawn, laid on the table, referred. or postponed.

5. A motion lost should not be recorded, except so ordered by the body at the time.

6. A motion lost cannot be renewed at the same meeting, except by unanimous consent.

7. A motion should contain but one distinct proposition. If it contains more, it must be divided at the request of any member, and the propositions acted on separately.

8. Only one question can properly be before the meeting at the same time. No second motion can be allowed to interrupt one already under debate, except a motion to *amend*, to *substitute*, to *commit*, to *postpone*, to *lay on the table*, for *the previous question*, or to *adjourn*.

9. These subsidiary motions just named cannot be interrupted by any other motion; nor can any other motion be applied to them, except that to *amend*, which may be done by specifying some *time*, *place*, or *purpose*.

10. Nor can these motions interrupt or supersede each other; only that a motion to *adjourn* is always in order, except while a member has the floor, or a question is being taken, and in some bodies even then.

Amendments.

1. Amendments may be made to resolutions in three ways: By *omitting*, by *adding*, or by *substituting* words or sentences.

2. An amendment to an amendment may be made, but is seldom necessary, and should be avoided.

3. No amendment should be made which essentially changes the meaning or design of the original resolution.

4. But a *substitute* may be offered, which may change entirely the meaning of the resolution under debate.

5. The amendment must first be discussed and acted on, and then the original resolution as amended.

Speaking.

1. Any member desiring to speak on a question should rise in his place, and address the moderator, confine his remarks to the question, and avoid all unkind and disrespectful language.

2. A speaker using improper language, introducing improper subjects, or otherwise out of order, should be called to order by the chairman, or any member, and must either conform to the regulations of the body, or take his seat.

3. A member while speaking can allow others to ask questions, or make explana-

tions; but if he yields the floor to another, he cannot claim it again as his right.

4. If two members rise to speak at the same time, preference is usually given to the one farthest from the chair, or to the one opposing the question under discussion.

5. The fact that a person has several times arisen, and attempted to get the floor, gives him no claim or right to be heard. Nor does a call for the question deprive a member of his right to speak.

Voting.

1. A question is put to vote by the chairman having first distinctly re-stated it, that all may vote intelligently. First, the *affirmative,* then the *negative* is called; each so deliberately as to give all an opportunity of voting. He then distinctly announces whether the motion is *carried,* or *lost.*

2. Voting is usually done by "aye" and "no," or by raising the hand. In a doubtful case by standing and being counted. On certain questions by ballot.

3. If the vote, as announced by the chairman, is doubted, it is called again, usually by standing to be counted.

4. All members should vote, unless for

reasons excused; or unless under discipline, in which case they should take no part in the business.

5. The moderator does not usually vote, except the question be taken by ballot; but when the meeting is equally divided, he is expected, but is not obliged to give the casting vote.

6. When the vote is to be taken by ballot, the chairman appoints *tellers*, to distribute, collect, and count the ballots.

Committees.

1. Committees are nominated by the chairman, if so directed by the body, or by any member; and the nomination is confirmed by a vote of the body. More commonly the body directs that all committees shall be *appointed* by the chairman, in which case no vote is needed to confirm.

2. Any matter of business, or subject under debate, may be *referred* to a committee, with or without instructions. The committee make their *report*, which is the result of their deliberations. The body then takes action on the report, and on any recommendations it may contain.

3. The report of a committee is *accepted*

by a vote, which acknowledges their services, and takes the report before the body for its action. Afterward, any distinct *recommendation* contained in the report is acted on, and may be adopted or rejected.

4. Frequently, however, when the recommendations of the committee are of a trifling moment or likely to be generally acceptable, the report is *accepted* and *adopted* by the same vote.

5. A report may be *recommitted* to the committee, with or without instructions; or that committee discharged, and the matter referred to a new one, for further consideration, so as to present it in a form more likely to meet the general concurrence of the body.

6. A committee may be appointed *with power* for a specific purpose. This gives them power to dispose conclusively of the matter, without further reference to the body.

7. The first named in the appointment of a committee is by courtesy considered the *chairman*. But the committee has the right to name its own chairman.

8. The member who moves the appointment of a committee is usually, though not necessarily, named its chairman.

9. Committees of arrangement, or for other protracted service, *report progress* from time to time, and are continued until their final report, or until their appointment expires by limitation.

10. A committee is *discharged* by a vote, when its business is done, and its report accepted. But usually, in routine business, a committee is considered discharged by the acceptance of its report.

Standing Committee.

A committee appointed to act for a given period or during the recess of the body is called a *standing committee.* It has charge of a given department of business assigned by the body, and acts either with power, under instructions, or at discretion, as may be ordered. A standing commiteee is substantially a minor board, and has its own chairman, secretary, records, and times of meeting.

Appeal.

The moderator announces all votes, and decides all questions as to rules of proceeding, and order of debate. But any member who is dissatisfied with his decisions may *appeal* from them to the body. The moderator then puts the question, "*Shall the decision of the chair be sustained?*" The vote of the body, whether negative or affirmative, is final. The right of appeal is undeniable, but should not be resorted to on trivial occasions.

Previous Question.

Debate may be cut short by a vote to take the *previous question.* This means that the original, or main question under discussion, be immediately voted on, regardless of amendments and secondary questions, and without further debate. Usually a *two-thirds* vote is necessary to order the previous question.

1. If the motion for the previous question be *carried,* then the main question must be immediately taken, without further debate.

2. If the motion for the previous question be *lost,* the debate proceeds, as though no such motion had been made.

3. If the motion for the previous question be *lost,* it cannot be renewed with reference to the same question, during the same session.

To Lay on the Table.

Immediate and decisive action on any question under discussion may be deferred, by a vote to *lay on the table* the resolution pending. This disposes of the whole subject for the present, and ordinarily is in effect a final dismissal of it. But any member has the right subsequently to call it up; and the body will decide by vote whether, or not, it shall be taken from the table.

1. Sometimes, however, a resolution is laid on the table for the present, or until a specified time, to give place to other business.

2. A motion to lay on the table must apply to a resolution, or other papers. An abstract subject cannot be disposed of in this way.

Postponement.

A simple *postponement* is for a specified time or purpose, the business to be resumed when the time or purpose is reached. But a question *indefinitely postponed* is considered as finally dismissed.

Not Debatable.

Certain motions, by established usage, are *not debatable,* but when once before the body, must be taken without discussion.

These are: The *previous question*, for *indefinite postponement*, to *commit*, to *lay on the table*, to *adjourn*.

But when these motions are modified by some condition of *time*, *place*, or *purpose*, they become debatable, and subject to the rules of other motions; but debatable only in respect to the time, place, or purpose which brings them within the province of debate.

A body is, however, competent, by a vote, to allow debate on all motions.

To Reconsider.

A motion to *reconsider* a motion previously passed must be made by one who voted *for* the motion when it passed.

If the body votes to reconsider, then the motion or resolution being reconsidered stands before them as previous to its passage, and may be discussed, adopted, or rejected.

A vote to reconsider should be taken at the same session at which the vote reconsidered was passed, and when there are as many members present.

Be Discussed.

If, when a question is introduced, any member objects to its discussion, as foreign, profitless, or contentious, the moderator should at once put the question, "*Shall this motion be discussed?*" If this question be decided in the negative, the subject must be dismissed.

Order of the Day.

The body may decide to take up some definite business at a specified time. That business therefore becomes the *order of the day*, for that hour. When the time mentioned arrives, the chairman calls the business, or any member may demand it, with or without a vote; and all pending questions are postponed in consequence.

Point of Order.

Any member who believes that a speaker is out of order, or that discussion is proceeding improperly, may at any time *rise to a point of order*. He must distinctly state his question or objection, which the moderator will decide.

Privileges.

Questions relating to the *rights* and *privileges* of members are of primary importance, and, until disposed of, take precedence of all other business, and supersede all other motions, except that of adjournment.

Rule Suspended.

A rule of order may be *suspended* by a vote of the body, to allow the transaction of business necessary, but which could not otherwise be done without a violation of such rule.

Filling Blanks.

Where different numbers are suggested for filling blanks, the *highest number*, *greatest distance*, and *longest time* are usually voted on first.

Adjournment.

1. A simple motion *to adjourn* is always in order, except while a member is speaking, or when taking a vote. It takes precedence of all other motions, and is not debatable.

2. In some deliberative bodies, a motion to adjourn is in order while a speaker has the floor, or a vote is being taken, the business to stand, on reassembling, precisely as when adjournment took place.

3. A body may adjourn to a specific

time; but if no time be mentioned, the fixed, or usual time of meeting, is understood. If there be no fixed, or usual time of meeting, then an adjournment without date is equivalent to a dissolution.

CHAPTER VIII.

CHRISTIAN DOCTRINE.

ALL evangelical churches profess to take the Holy Scriptures as their only and sufficient guide in matters of religious faith and practice. Baptists, especially, claim to have no authoritative creed except the New Testament. It is common, however, for the churches to have formulated statements of what are understood to be the leading Christian doctrines, printed and circulated among their members. These are not uniform among the churches, but are in substantial agreement as to the doctrines taught. Indeed, each church is at liberty to prepare its own confession, or have none at all; no one form being held as binding and obligatory on the churches to adopt. Members, on being received to fellowship, are not required to subscribe or pledge conformity to any creed-form, but are expected to yield substantial agreement to that which the church with which they unite has adopted.

There are two Confessions which have gained more general acceptance than any others, and are now being widely adopted by the churches over the country. As to substance of doctrine, they do not essentially differ. That known as the New Hampshire Confession is commonly used by the churches North, East. and West; while that known as the Philadelphia Confession, is very generally in use in the South and Southwest. The former is much more brief, and for that reason preferred by many. The other is substantially the London Confession of Faith, published by English Baptists in 1689. It is much more full in statement than the other, and is higher in its tone as to the doctrines of grace.

American Baptists are decidedly Calvinistic as to substance of doctrine, but moderately so, being midway between the extremes of Arminianism and Antinomianism. Though diversities of opinion may incline to either extreme, the "general atonement" view is for the most part held, while the "particular atonement" theory is maintained by not a few. The freedom of the human will is declared, while the sovereignty of divine grace, and the absolute necessity of the

Spirit's work in faith and salvation are maintained. They practice "strict communion," as do their mission churches in foreign lands. In Great Britain Baptists are sharply divided between "strict and free communion," and between the particular and the general atonement theories.

The New Hampshire Confession, with a few verbal changes, is here inserted. A part of the proof texts usually accompanying these articles are, for want of space, omitted.[1]

ARTICLES OF FAITH.

I. THE SCRIPTURES.

We believe that the Holy Bible was written by men divinely inspired, and is a perfect treasure of heavenly instruction;[1] that it has God for its author, salvation for its end, and truth without any mixture of error for its matter;[2] that it reveals the principles by which God will judge us;[3] and therefore is, and shall remain to the end of the world, the true centre of Christian union, and the

---

[1] For a fuller account of these Confessions, see the "Baptist Church Directory."

supreme standard by which all human conduct, creeds, and opinions should be tried.

[1] 2 Tim. 3 : 16, 17. All Scripture is given by inspiration of God, and is profitable for doctrine, for reproof, for correction, for instruction in righteousness; that the man of God may be perfect, thoroughly furnished unto all good works. Also, 2 Pet. 1 : 21; 2 Sam. 23 : 2; Acts 1 : 16.

[2] Prov. 30 : 5, 6. Every word of God is pure. Add thou not unto his words, lest he reprove thee, and thou be found a liar. Also, John 17 : 17; Rev. 22 : 18, 19; Rom. 3 : 4.

[3] Rom. 2 : 12. As many as have sinned in the law, shall be judged by the law. John 12 : 47, 48. If any man hear my words—the word that I have spoken, the same shall judge him in the last day. Also, 1 Cor. 4 : 3, 4; Luke 10 : 10–16; 12 : 47, 48

II. THE TRUE GOD.

We believe the Scriptures teach that there is one, and only one, living and true God, an infinite, intelligent Spirit, whose name is JEHOVAH, the Maker and Supreme Ruler of Heaven and Earth:[1] inexpressibly glorious in holiness,[2] and worthy of all possible honor, confidence, and love;[3] that in the unity of the Godhead there are three persons, the Father, the Son, and the Holy Ghost;[4] equal in every divine perfection, and executing distinct but harmonious offices in the great work of redemption.

[1] John 4 : 24. God is a Spirit. Ps. 147 : 5. His understanding is infinite. Ps. 83 : 18. Thou whose name alone is JEHOVAH, art the Most High over all the earth. Heb. 3 : 4; Rom. 1 : 20; Jer. 10 : 10.

[2] Exod. 15 : 11. Who is like unto thee—glorious in holiness? Isa. 6 : 3; 1 Peter 1 : 15, 16; Rev. 4 : 6–8.

[3] Mark 12 : 30. Thou shalt love the Lord thy God with all thy heart, and with all thy soul, and with all thy mind, and with all thy strength. Rev. 4 : 11. Thou art worthy, O Lord to receive glory, and honour, and power. Matt. 10 : 37 ; Jer. 2 : 12, 13.

[4] Matt. 28 : 19. Go ye therefore and teach all nations, baptizing them in the name of the Father, and of the Son, and of the Holy Ghost. John 15 : 26 ; 1 Cor. 12 : 4-6.

III. THE FALL OF MAN.

We believe the Scriptures teach that man was created in holiness, under the law of his Maker ;[1] but by voluntary transgresson fell from that holy and happy state ;[2] in consequence of which all mankind are now sinners,[3] not by constraint but choice ; being by nature utterly void of that holiness required by the law of God, positively inclined to evil ; and therefore under just condemnation[4] without defense or excuse.[5]

[1] Gen. 1 : 27. God created man in his own image. Gen 1 : 31. And God saw everything that he had made, and behold, it was very good. Eccl. 7 : 29 ; Acts 17 : 26 ; Gen. 2 : 16.

[2] Gen. 3 : 6-24. And when the woman saw that the tree was good for food, and that it was pleasant to the eyes, and a tree to be desired to make one wise ; she took of the fruit thereof, and did eat ; and gave also unto her husband with her, and he did eat. Rom. 5 : 12.

[3] Rom. 5 : 19. By one man's disobedience many were made sinners. John 3 : 6 ; Ps. 51 : 5 ; Rom. 5 : 15-19 ; 8 : 7.

[4] Eph. 2 : 3. Among whom also we all had our conversation in times past in the lusts of our flesh, fulfilling the desires of the flesh and of the mind ; and were by nature the children of wrath even as others.

[5] Ezek. 18 : 19, 20. The soul that sinneth it shall die. Rom. 1 : 20. So that they are without excuse. Rom. 3 : 19. That every mouth may be stopped and all the world may become guilty before God. Gal. 3 : 22.

IV. THE WAY OF SALVATION.

We believe the Scriptures teach that the salvation of sinners is wholly of grace;[1] through the mediatorial offices of the Son of God;[2] who, according to the will of the Father, became man, yet without sin;[3] honored the divine law by his personal obedience, and by his death made a full atonement for our sins;[4] that having risen from the dead, he is now enthroned in heaven; and uniting in his wonderful person the tenderest sympathies with divine perfections, he is every way qualified to be a suitable, a compassionate and an all-sufficient Saviour.[5]

[1] Eph. 2: 5. By grace ye are saved. Matt. 18: 11; 1 John 4: 10; 1 Cor. 3: 5-7; Acts 15: 11.

[2] John 3: 16. For God so loved the world that he gave his only begotten Son, that whosoever believeth in him should not perish, but have everlasting life.

[3] Phil. 2: 6, 7. Who being in the form of God, thought it not robbery to be equal with God; but made himself of no reputation, and took upon him the form of a servant, and was made in the likeness of men.

[4] Isa. 53: 4, 5. He was wounded for our transgressions, he was bruised for our iniquities; the chastisement of our peace was upon him; and with his stripes we are healed.

[5] Heb. 7: 25. Wherefore he is able also to save them to the uttermost that come unto God by him, seeing he ever liveth to make intercession for them. Col. 2: 9. For in him dwelleth all the fulness of the Godhead bodily.

V. JUSTIFICATION.

We believe the Scriptures teach that the great gospel blessing which Christ[1] secures to such as believe in him is justification;[2] that justification includes the pardon of sin,[3] and the gift of eternal life on principles of righteousness; that it is bestowed, not in consideration of any works of righteousness which we have done, but solely through faith in Christ; by means of which faith his perfect righteousness is freely imputed to us by God;[4] that it brings us into a state of most blessed peace and favor with God, and secures every other blessing needful for time and eternity.[5]

[1] John 1:16. Of his fulness have all we received. Eph. 3:8.

[2] Acts 13:39. By him all that believe are justified from all things. Isa. 3:11, 12; Rom. 5:1.

[3] Rom. 5:9. Being justified by his blood, we shall be saved from wrath through him. Zech. 13:1; Matt. 9:6; Acts 10:43

[4] Rom. 5:19. By the obedience of one shall many be made righteous. Rom. 3:24-26; 4:23-25; 1 John 2:12.

[5] Rom. 5:1, 2. Being justified by faith, we have peace with God, through our Lord Jesus Christ; by whom also we have access by faith into this grace wherein we stand, and rejoice in hope of the glory of God.

VI. THE FREENESS OF SALVATION.

We believe the Scriptures teach that the blessings of salvation are made free to all by the gospel:[1] that it is the immediate duty of all to accept them by a cordial, penitent, and obedient faith;[2] and that nothing prevents the salvation of the greatest sinner on earth but his own determined depravity and voluntary rejection of the gospel;[3] which rejection involves him in an aggravated condemnation.[4]

[1] Isa. 55: 1. Ho, every one that thirsteth, come ye to the waters. Rev. 22: 17. Whosoever will let him take the water of life freely.

[2] Acts 17: 30. And the times of this ignorance God winked at, but now commandeth all men everywhere to repent. Rom. 16: 26; Mark 1: 15; Rom. 1: 15–17.

[3] John 5: 40. Ye will not come to me, that ye might have life. Matt. 23: 37; Rom. 9: 32.

[4] John 3: 19. And this is the condemnation, that light is come into the world, and men loved darkness rather than light because their deeds were evil. Matt. 11: 20; Luke 19: 27; 2 Thess. 1: 8.

VII. REGENERATION.

We believe the Scriptures teach that in order to be saved, men must be regenerated, or born again;[1] that regeneration consists in giving a holy disposition to the mind;[2] that it is effected in a manner above our comprehension by the Holy Spirit, in connection with divine truth,[3] so as to secure our voluntary obedience to the gospel;[4] and that its proper evidence appears in the holy fruits of repentance, faith, and newness of life.[5]

[1] John 3: 3. Verily, verily, I say unto thee, except a man be born again, he cannot see the kingdom of God. John 3: 6, 7; 1 Cor. 1: 14; Rev. 8 : 7–9; Rev. 21: 27.

[2] 2 Cor. 5: 17. If any man be in Christ, he is a new creature. Ezek. 36: 26; Deut. 30: 6; Rom. 2: 28, 29.

[3] John 3: 8. The wind bloweth where it listeth, and thou hearest the sound thereof, but canst not tell whence it cometh, and whither it goeth; so is every one that is born of the Spirit. John 1: 13; James 1: 16–18; 1 Cor. 1: 30; Phil. 2: 13.

[4] 1 Peter 1: 22: 25. Ye have purified your souls in obeying the truth through the Spirit. 1 John 5: 1; Eph. 4: 20–24; Col. 3: 9–11.

[5] Eph. 5: 9. The fruit of the Spirit is in all goodness and righteousness, and truth. Rom. 8: 9; Gal. 5: 16–23; Eph. 3: 14–21; Matt. 3: 8–10; 7: 20; 1 John 5: 4, 18.

VIII. REPENTANCE AND FAITH.

We believe the Scriptures teach that repentance and faith are sacred duties, and also inseparable graces, wrought in the soul by the regenerating Spirit of God;[1] whereby being deeply convinced of our guilt, danger, and helplessness, and of the way of salvation by Christ,[2] we turn to God with unfeigned contrition, confession, and supplication for mercy; at the same time heartily receiving the Lord Jesus as our prophet, priest, and king, and relying on him alone as the only and all-sufficient Saviour.[3]

[1] Mark 1: 15. Repent ye, and believe the gospel. Acts 11: 18. Then hath God also to the Gentiles granted repentance

unto life. Eph. 2 : 8. By grace ye are saved, through faith; and that not of yourselves; it is the gift of God. 1 John 5 : 1.

[2] John 16 : 8. He will reprove the world of sin, and of righteousness, and of judgment. Acts 11 : 38. Then Peter said unto them, Repent, and be baptized every one of you in the name of Jesus Christ for the remission of sins. Acts 16 : 30, 31.

[3] Romans 10 : 9–11. If thou shalt confess with thy mouth the Lord Jesus, and shalt believe in thy heart that God hath raised him from the dead, thou shalt be saved. Acts 3 : 22, 23; Heb. 4 : 14.

IX. GOD'S PURPOSE OF GRACE.

We believe the Scriptures teach that election is the eternal purpose of God, according to which he graciously regenerates, sanctifies, and saves sinners;[1] that being perfectly consistent with the free agency of man, it comprehends all the means in connection with the end;[2] that it is a most glorious display of God's sovereign goodness;[3] that it utterly excludes boasting, and promotes humility;[4] that it encourages the use of means; that it may be ascertained by its effects in all who truly accept of Christ[5]; that it is the foundation of Christian assurance; and that to ascertain it with regard to ourselves demands and deserves the utmost diligence.[6]

[1] 2 Tim 1 : 8, 9. But be thou partaker of the afflictions of the gospel, according to the power of God; who hath saved us and called us with a holy calling, not according to our works, but according to his own purpose and grace which was given us in Christ Jesus before the world began.

[2] 2 Thess. 2 : 13, 14. But we are bound to give thanks always to God for you, brethren beloved of the Lord, because God hath from the beginning chosen you to salvation, through sanctification of the Spirit and belief of the truth; whereunto he called you by our gospel, to the obtaining of the glory of our Lord Jesus Christ.

[3] 1 Cor. 4 : 7. For who maketh thee to differ from another? and what hast thou that thou didst not receive? Now if thou didst receive it, why dost thou glory as if thou hadst not received it? 1 Cor. 1 : 26–31; Rom. 3 : 27.

[4] 2 Tim 2 : 10. Therefore I endure all things for the elects' sake, that they also may obtain the salvation which is in Christ Jesus with eternal glory. 1 Cor. 9 : 22; Rom. 8 : 28–30.

[5] 1 Thess. 4 : 10. Knowing, brethren beloved, your election of God.

[6] 2 Peter 1 : 10, 11. Wherefore the rather, brethren, give diligence to make your calling and election sure. Phil. 3 : 12; Heb. 6 : 11.

X. SANCTIFICATION.

We believe the Scriptures teach that sanctification is the process by which, according to the will of God, we are made partakers of his holiness;[1] that it is a progressive work;[2] that it is begun in regeneration; that it is carried on in the hearts of believers by the presence and power of the Holy Spirit, the Sealer and Comforter, in the continual use of the appointed means—especially the word of God—self-examination, self-denial, watchfulness, and prayer;[3] and in the practice of all godly exercises and duties.[4]

[1] 1 Thess. 4 : 3. For this is the will of God, even your sanctification. 1 Thess. 5 : 23. And the very God of peace sanctify you wholly. 2 Cor. 7 : 1; 13 : 9; Eph. 1 : 4.

[2] Prov. 4 : 18. The path of the just is as the shining light, which shineth more and more, unto the perfect day.

[3] Phil. 1 : 12, 13. Work out your own salvation with fear and trembling, for it is God which worketh in you both to will and to do, of his good pleasure. Eph. 4 : 11, 12; 1 Peter 2 : 2; 2 Peter 3 : 18; 2 Cor. 13 : 5; Luke 11 : 35; 9 : 23; Matt. 26 : 41; Eph. 6 : 18; 4 : 30.

[4] 1 Tim 4 : 7. Exercise thyself unto godliness.

XI. PERSEVERANCE OF SAINTS.

We believe the Scriptures teach that such as are truly regenerate, being born of the Spirit, will not utterly fall away and perish, but will endure unto the end;[1] that their persevering attachment to Christ is the grand mark which distinguishes them from superficial professors;[2] that a special Providence watches over their welfare;[3] and that they are kept by the power of God through faith unto salvation.[4]

[1] John 8 : 31. Then said Jesus, If ye contiue in my word, then are ye my disciples indeed. 1 John 2 : 27, 28.

[2] John 2 : 19. They went out from us, but they were not of us; for if they had been of us, they would no doubt have continued with us; but they went out that it might be made manifest that they were not all of us.

[3] Rom. 8 : 28. And we know all things work together for good unto them that love God, to them who are the called according to his purpose. Matt. 6 : 30-33; Jer. 32 : 40.

[4] Phil. 1 : 6. He who hath begun a good work in you will perform it until the day of Jesus Christ. Phil. 2 : 12, 13.

XII. THE LAW AND GOSPEL.

We believe the Scriptures teach that the law of God is the eternal and unchangeable rule of his moral government;[1] that it is holy, just, and good;[2] and that the inability which the Scriptures ascribe to fallen men to fulfill its precepts arises entirely from their sinful nature;[3] to deliver them from which, and to restore them through a Mediator to unfeigned obedience to the holy law, is one great end of the gospel, and of the means of grace connected with the establishment of the visible church.[4]

[1] Rom. 3 : 31. Do we make void the law through faith? God forbid. Yea, we establish the law. Matt. 5 : 17; Luke 16 : 17; Rom. 3 : 20; 4 : 15.

[2] Rom. 7 : 12. The law is holy, and the commandment holy, and just, and good. Rom. 7 : 7, 14, 22; Gal. 3 : 21; Ps. 119.

[3] Rom. 8 : 7, 8. The carnal mind is enmity against God; for it is not subject to the law of God, neither indeed can be. So then they that are in the flesh cannot please God.

[4] Rom. 8 : 2, 4. For the law of the Spirit of life in Christ Jesus hath made me free from the law of sin and death. For what the law could not do, in that it was weak through the flesh, God sending his own Son in the likeness of sinful flesh, and for sin, condemned sin in the flesh: that the righteousness of the law might be fulfilled in us, who walk not after the flesh, but after the Spirit.

XIII. A GOSPEL CHURCH.

We believe the Scriptures teach that a visible Church of Christ is a company of baptized believers,[1] associated by covenant in the faith and fellowship of the gospel;[2] observing the ordinances of Christ;[3] governed by his laws;[4] and exercising the gifts, rights, and privileges invested in them by his word;[5] that its only scriptural officers are bishops or pastors, and deacons,[6] whose qualifications, claims, and duties are defined in the Epistles to Timothy and Titus.

[1] Acts 2 : 41, 42. Then they that gladly received his word were baptized; and the same day there were added to them about three thousand souls.

[2] 2 Cor. 8 : 5. They first gave their own selves to the Lord, and unto us by the will of God.

[3] 1 Cor. 11 : 2. Now I praise you, brethren, that ye remember me in all things, and keep the ordinances as I delivered them to you.

[4] Matt. 28 : 20. Teaching them to observe all things whatsoever I have commanded you. John 14 : 15.

[5] 1 Cor. 14 : 12. Seek that ye may excel to the edifying of the church.

[6] Phil. 1 : 1. With the bishops and deacons. Acts 14 : 23; 15 : 22. 1 Tim. 3. Titus 1.

XIV. CHRISTIAN BAPTISM.

We believe the Scriptures teach that Christian baptism is the immersion in water of a believer in Christ,[1] into the name of the Father, and Son, and Holy Ghost;[2] to show forth in a solemn and beautiful emblem his faith in the crucified, buried, and risen Saviour, with its effect, in his death to sin and resurrection to a new life;[3] that it is prerequisite to the privileges of a church relation, and to the Lord's Supper.[4]

[1] Acts 8 : 36–39. And the eunuch said, See, here is water; what doth hinder me to be baptized? And Philip said, If thou believest with all thy heart, thou mayest. . . . And they went down into the water, both Philip and the eunuch, and he baptized him. Matt. 3 : 5, 6; John 3 : 22, 23; 4 : 1, 2; Matt. 28 : 19.

[2] Matt. 18 : 19. Baptizing them in the name of the Father, and of the Son, and of the Holy Ghost. Acts 10 : 47, 48: Gal. 3 : 27, 28.

[3] Rom. 6 : 4. Therefore we are buried with him by baptism into death; that like as Christ was raised from the dead by the glory of the Father, even so we also, should walk in newness of life. Col. 2 : 12.

[4] Acts 2 : 41, 42. Then they that gladly received his word were baptized, and there were added to them, the same day, about three thousand souls. And they continued steadfastly in the apostles' doctrine and fellowship, and in breaking of bread, and in prayers. Matt. 28 : 19, 20.

XV. THE LORD'S SUPPER.

We believe the Scriptures teach that the Lord's Supper is a provision of bread and wine, representing Christ's body and blood, partaken of by the members of the church assembled for that purpose,[1] in commemoration of the death of their Lord,[2] showing their faith and participation in the merits of his sacrifice, their dependence on him for spiritual life and nourishment,[3] and their hope of life eternal through his resurrection from the dead; its observance to be preceded by faithful self-examination.[4]

[1] Luke 22 : 19, 20. And he took bread, and gave thanks and brake, and gave unto them, saying, This is my body, which is given for you; this do in remembrance of me. Likewise the cup after supper, saying, This cup is the new testament in my blood, which is shed for you. Mark 14 : 20–26; Matt. 26 : 27–30; 1 Cor. 11 : 27–30; 1 Cor. 10 : 16.

[2] 1 Cor. 11 : 26. For as oft as ye eat this bread, and drink this cup, ye do shew the Lord's death until he come. Matt. 28 : 20.

[3] John 6 : 35, 54, 56. Jesus said unto them, I am the bread of life. Whoso eateth my flesh and drinketh my blood hath eternal life. He that eateth my flesh and drinketh my blood dwelleth in me, and I in him.

[4] 1 Cor. 11 : 28. But let a man examine himself, and so let him eat of that bread, and drink of that cup. Acts 2 : 42, 46; 20 : 7, 11.

XVI. THE LORD'S DAY.

We believe the Scriptures teach that the first day of the week is the Lord's Day,[1] and is to be kept sacred to religious purposes[2] by abstaining from all secular labor, except works of mercy and necessity;[3] by the devout observance of all the means of grace, both private and public;[4] and by preparation for that rest that remaineth for the people of God.

[1] Acts 20 : 7. On the first day of the week, when the disciples came together to break bread, Paul preached to them.

[2] Exod. 20 : 8. Remember the Sabbath Day, to keep it holy. Rev. 1 : 10. I was in the Spirit on the Lord's Day. Ps. 118 : 24.

[3] Isa. 58 : 13, 14. If thou turn away thy foot from the Sabbath, from doing thy pleasure on my holy day; and call the Sabbath a delight, the holy of the Lord honourable; and shalt honour him, not doing thine own ways, nor finding thine own pleasure, nor speaking thine own words; then shall thou delight thyself in the Lord, and I will cause thee to ride upon the high places of the earth, and feed thee with the heritage of Jacob. Isa. 56 : 2–8.

[4] Heb. 10 : 24, 25. Not forsaking the assembling of yourselves together, as the manner of some is. Acts 13 : 44. The next Sabbath Day came almost the whole city together to hear the word of God.

XVII. CIVIL GOVERNMENT.

We believe the Scriptures teach that civil government is of divine appointment, for the interest and good order of human society;[1] and that magistrates are to be prayed for, conscientiously honored, and obeyed;[2] except only in things opposed to the will of our Lord Jesus Christ,[3] who is the only Lord of the conscience, and the Prince of the kings of the earth.[4]

[1] Rom. 13 : 1–7. The powers that be are ordained of God. For rulers are not a terror to good works, but to the evil.

[2] Matt. 22 : 21. Render therefore unto Cæsar the things that are Cæsar's, and unto God the things that are God's. Titus 3 : 1; 1 Peter 2 : 13; 1 Tim. 2 : 1–8.

[3] Acts 5 : 29. We ought to obey God rather than man. Matt. 10 : 28. Fear not them which kill the body, but are not able to kill the soul. Dan. 3 : 15–18; 6 : 7, 10; Acts 4 : 18–20.

[4] Matt. 23 : 10. Ye have one Master, even Christ. Rev. 19 : 14. And he hath on his vesture and on his thigh a name written, KING OF KINGS AND LORD OF LORDS. Ps. 72 : 11; Ps. 2; Rom. 14 : 9–13.

XVIII. RIGHTEOUS AND WICKED.

We believe the Scriptures teach that there is a radical and essential difference between the righteous and the wicked;[1] that such only as are regenerate, being justified through faith in Jesus Christ and sanctified by the Spirit of God, are truly righteous in his esteem;[2] while all such as continue in impenitence and unbelief are, in his sight, wicked and under the curse;[3] and this distinction holds among men, both in and after death.[4]

[1] Mal. 3 : 18. Ye shall discern between the righteous and the wicked; between him that serveth God and him that serveth him not. Prov. 12 : 26; Isa. 5 : 20; Gen. 18 : 23; Jer. 15 : 19; Acts 10 : 34, 35; Rom. 6 : 16.

[2] Rom. 1 : 17. The just shall live by faith. 1 John 2 : 29. If ye know that he is righteous, ye know that every one that doeth righteousness is born of him. 1 John 3 : 7; Rom. 6 : 18, 22; 1 Cor. 11 : 32; Prov. 11 : 31; 1 Peter 4 : 17, 18.

[3] 1 John 5 : 19. And we know that we are of God, and the whole world lieth in wickedness. Gal. 3 : 10. As many as are of the works of the law, are under the curse. John 3 : 36; Isa. 57 : 21; Ps. 10 : 4; Isa. 55 : 6, 7.

[4] Prov. 14 : 32. The wicked is driven away in his wickedness, but the righteous hath hope in his death. Luke 16 : 25. Thou in thy lifetime receivedst thy good things, and likewise Lazarus evil things; but now he is comforted, and thou art tormented. John 8 : 21–24; Prov. 10 : 24; Luke 12 : 4, 5; 11 : 23–26; John 12 : 25, 26; Eccl. 3 : 17.

XIX. THE WORLD TO COME.

We believe the Scriptures teach that the end of the world is approaching;[1] that at the last day Christ will descend from heaven,[2] and raise the dead from the grave for final retribution;[3] that a solemn separation will then take place;[4] that the wicked will be adjudged to endless sorrow, and the righteous to endless joy;[5] and that this judgment will fix forever the final state of men in heaven or hell on principles of righteousness.[6]

[1] 1 Peter 4 : 7. But the end of all things is at hand; be ye therefore sober, and watch unto prayer. 1 Cor. 7 : 29–31; Heb. 1 : 10–12; Matt. 24 : 35.

[2] Acts 1 : 11. This same Jesus which is taken up from you into heaven, shall so come in like manner as ye have seen him go into heaven.

[3] Acts 24 : 15. There shall be a resurrection of the dead, both of the just and unjust. 1 Cor. 15 : 12–58; Luke 14 : 14; Dan. 12 : 2.

[4] Matt. 13 : 49. The angels shall come forth, and sever the wicked from among the just. Matt. 13 : 37–43; 24 : 30, 31; 25 : 31–33.

[5] Matt. 25 : 35–41. And these shall go away into everlasting punishment, but the righteous into life eternal. Rev. 22 : 11. He that is unjust, let him be unjust still; and he which is filthy, let him be filthy still; and he that is righteous, let him be righteous still; and he that is holy, let him be holy still. 1 Cor. 6 : 9, 10; Mark 9 : 43–48.

[6] 2 Thess. 1 : 6–12. Seeing it is a righteous thing with God to recompense tribulations to them who trouble you, and to you who are troubled, rest with us . . . when he shall come to be glorified in his saints, and to be admired in all them that believe. Heb. 6 : 1, 2; 1 Cor. 4 : 5; Acts 17 : 31; Rom. 2 : 2-16, Rev. 20 : 11, 12; 1 John 2 : 28; 4 : 17. 2 Peter 3 : 11, 12. Seeing then that all these things shall be dissolved, what manner of persons ought ye to be in all holy conversation and godliness, looking for and hasting unto the coming of the day of God?

COVENANT.

Having been, as we trust, brought by divine grace to embrace the Lord Jesus Christ, and to give ourselves wholly to him, we do now solemnly and joyfully covenant with each other TO WALK TOGETHER IN HIM, WITH BROTHERLY LOVE, to his glory, as our common Lord. We do, therefore, in his strength, engage—

That we will exercise a Christian care and watchfulness over each other, and faithfully warn, exhort, and admonish each other as occasion may require:

That we will not forsake the assembling of ourselves together, but will uphold the public worship of God and the ordinances of his house:

That we will not omit closet and family religion at home, nor neglect the great duty of religiously training our children, and those under our care, for the service of Christ and the enjoyment of heaven:

That, as we are the light of the world, and the salt of the earth, we will seek divine aid, to enable us to deny ungodliness and every worldly lust, and to walk circumspectly in the world, that we may win the souls of men:

That we will cheerfully contribute of our property, according as God has prospered us, for the maintenance of a faithful and evangelical ministry among us, for the support of the poor, and to spread the gospel over the earth:

That we will in all conditions, even till

death, strive to live to the glory of him who hath called us out of darkness into his marvelous light.

"And may the God of peace, who brought again from the dead our Lord Jesus, that great Shepherd of the sheep, through the blood of the everlasting covenant, make us perfect in every good work to do his will, working in us that which is well pleasing in his sight through Jesus Christ, to whom be glory, for ever and ever. Amen."

CHAPTER IX.

OPTIONAL STANDING RESOLUTIONS.

A CHRISTIAN church should be the uncompromising friend of all virtue, and the determined enemy of all vice. Public morality and social purity should find in it an open and earnest advocate and defender. Churches should bear in mind that Christian morality, which constitutes their rule of life, claims a much higher standard than the morality of worldly society about them. Therefore their deportment should be such as to have a good report of them that are without, and command the respect of the world. In all this the pastor should be the wise but decided and courageous teacher, leader and exemplar for his people.

There are certain questions of moral reform and social recreation with reference to which the churches are often much perplexed, but with reference to which they should have settled convictions, and hold a well-defined attitude. It is not wise to put definitions and restrictions touching intemperance, card playing, theatre going, dancing, and the like, into covenants or articles of faith. A better way is for the church, after due consideration, to pass *standing resolutions* on the subject, to be placed on its records as a guide to future action. Something like the following, to be varied at the option of the body, would serve as a declaration of principles:

1. *Resolved,* That this church expects every member to contribute statedly for its pecuniary support, according to his ability, as God has prospered him, and that a refusal to do this will be considered a breach of covenant.

2. *Resolved,* That this church will entertain and contribute statedly to Home and Foreign Missions, and to other leading objects of Christian benevolence, approved of and supported by our denomination.

3. *Resolved,* That the religious education of the young and Bible study as represented in Sunday-school work commend themselves to our confidence, and we will, to the extent of our ability, give them our sympathy and our aid, by both our personal

co-operation and contributions, and expressed appreciation of all their legitimate aims and work.

4. *Resolved,* That in our opinion, the use of intoxicating drinks as a beverage, and also the manufacture and sale of the same for such a purpose, are contrary to Christian morals, injurious to personal piety, and a hindrance to gospel truth, and that persons so using, making or selling, are thereby disqualified for membership in this church.

5. *Resolved,* That we emphatically discountenance and condemn the practice of church members frequenting theatres and other similar places of public amusements, as inconsistent with a Christian profession, detrimental to personal piety, and pernicious in the influence of its example on others.

6. *Resolved,* That the members of this church are earnestly requested not to provide for, take part in, or by any means encourage dancing or card playing; but in all consistent ways to discountenance the same as a hindrance to personal godliness in their associations and tendencies. and an offense to brethren whom we should not willingly grieve.

CHAPTER X.

BAPTISM CONSIDERED.

WHAT is Christian baptism? This is the gravest question which enters into the baptismal controversy. Other questions of moment there are in connection with it, touching the design, the efficacy, and the subjects. But it is of primary importance to know what constitutes baptism.

Baptists answer the question by saying that baptism is the immersion, dipping, or burying in water, of a professed believer in Christ, in the name of the Father, the Son, and the Holy Spirit.

Pedobaptists, both Roman Catholic and Protestant, answer the question by saying that baptism is either the sprinkling or pouring of water upon the candidate, touching the forehead with wet fingers, or dipping the person wholly into water; in either case in the name of the Father, the Son, and the Spirit; and that it may be administered to a candidate on his profession of faith, or to an unconscious infant on the professed faith of parents or sponsors. This would make four kinds of baptism, and two classes of subjects for its reception; and would consist rather in the application of water to the person, than putting the person into water.

Baptists hold to a unity of the ordinance, as well as to a oneness of the faith; insisting that as there is but one Lord, and one faith, so there is but one baptism. And the dipping in water of a professed disciple of Christ is that one baptism. Neither sprinkling a person with water, nor pouring water upon him can by any possibility be Christian baptism. That this position is the true one, we appeal to the New Testament, and the best extant historical and philological authorities to establish.

Let it be distinctly understood, however, that all the eminent names and learned authorities hereafter cited are Pedobaptists. Baptist authorities are wholly omitted, not because they are less accurate or less valuable, but because we prefer to allow our opponents in this controversy to bear witness for us, rather than to testify in our own behalf.

MEANING OF THE WORD.

The word *baptize* is, properly speaking, a Greek word (*baptizo*), adapted to the English language by a change in its termination. This is the word always used by Christ and his apostles to express and define the ordinance. What does that word mean, as originally used? For it is certain that our Lord, in commanding a rite to be observed by believers of all classes, in all lands, and through all ages, would use a word of positive and definite import, and one whose meaning would admit of no reasonable doubt. What do Greek scholars say? How do the Greek lexicons define the word?

SCAPULA says: "To *dip*, to immerse, as we do anything for the purpose of dyeing it."

SCHLEUSNER says: "Properly it signifies to *dip*, to immerse, to immerse in water."

PARKHURST says: "To dip, *immerse*, or plunge in water."

STEVENS says: "To merge, or *immerse*, to submerge, or bury in water."

DONNEGAN says: "To *immerse* repeatedly into liquid, to submerge, to soak thoroughly."

ROBINSON says: "To *immerse*, to sink."

LIDDELL AND SCOTT say: "To *dip* repeatedly."

GRIMM'S LEXICON *of the New Testament*, which in Europe and America stands confessedly at the head of Greek lexicography, as translated and edited by Professor Thayer, of Harvard University, thus defines *baptizo:* "(1) To dip repeatedly, to immerse, submerge. (2) To cleanse by dipping or submerging. (3) To overwhelm. In the New Testament it is used particularly of the rite of sacred ablution; first instituted by John the Baptist, afterward by Christ's command received by Christians and adjusted to the contents and nature of their religion, viz., an *immersion* in water, performed as a sign of the removal of sin, and administered to those who, impelled by a desire for salvation, sought admission to the benefits of the Messiah's kingdom. With *eis* to mark the element into which the immersion is made; *en* with the dative of the thing in which one is immersed."

The noun *baptisma*, the only other word used in the New Testament to denote the rite, GRIMM-THAYER thus define: "A word peculiar to the New Testament and ecclesiastical writers; used (1) of John's baptism; (2) of Christian baptism. This, according to the view of the Apostles, is a rite of sacred *immersion* commanded by Christ."

Add to those such authorities as Alstidius, Passow, Schöttgen, Stockius, Stourdza, Sophocles, Anthon, Rosenmüller, Wetstein, Leigh, Turretin, Beza, Calvin, Witsius, Luther, Vossius, Campbell, and many others who bear the same witness to the proper meaning of the word *baptize.* If at any time the word may have a secondary meaning, it is strictly in accord with its primary meaning—to dip, or immerse. For both classic and sacred Greek the same meaning holds.

PROF. MOSES STUART, one of the ablest scholars America has produced, declared: "*Baptizo* means to dip, plunge, or *immerse* into any liquid. All lexicographers and critics of any note are agreed in this." *Essay on Baptism, p. 51; Biblical Repository, 1833, p. 298.*

"All lexicographers and critics, of any note, are agreed in this," says one of the foremost scholars of the age, and he a Pedobaptist. What a concession!

The Greek language is rich in terms for the expression of all positive ideas, and all varying shades of thought. Why, then, did our Lord in commanding, and his Apostles in transmitting his command to posterity, use *always* and *only* that one word *baptizo,* to describe the action, and that one word *baptizma,* to describe the ordinance to which he intended all his followers to submit? The word *louo* means to *wash* the body, and *uipto* to wash parts of the body; but these words are not used, because washing is not what Christ meant. *Rantizo* means to *sprinkle,* and if sprinkling were baptism this would have been the word above all others; but it was never so used. *Keo* means to *pour;* but pouring is not baptism, and so this word was never used to describe the ordinance. *Katharizo* means to *purify,* but is not used for the ordinance. The facts are clear and the reasoning conclusive.

STOURDZA, the Russian scholar and diplomat, says: "The church of the West has then departed from the example of Jesus Christ; she has obliterated the whole sublimity of the exterior sign. Baptism and immersion are *identical.* Baptism by *aspersion* is as if one should say *immersion* by

8

aspersion, or any other absurdity of the same nature." *Considerations, Orthodox Ch., p. 87.*

THE BAPTISM OF JESUS.

The baptism of Jesus in the Jordan is thus described: "And Jesus, when he was baptized, went up straightway out of the water." (Matt. 3 : 16.) And again, it is recorded that Jesus "was baptized of John in Jordan; and straightway coming up out of the water." (Mark 1 : 10.) He certainly would not go down into Jordan to have water sprinkled on him. Nobody believes he would. He was baptized *in* Jordan, not *with* Jordan. Moreover, he was *baptized*, that is, *immersed*, not *rantized*, that is, *sprinkled*.

Bishop Taylor says: "The custom of the ancient churches was not sprinkling, but *immersion*, in pursuance of the meaning of the word in the commandments and the example of our blessed Saviour." *Commentary on Matthew 3 : 16.*

MacKnight says: "Christ submitted to be baptized, that is, to be *buried* under water, and to be raised out of it again, as an emblem of his future death and resurrection." *Com. Epis., Rom. 6 : 4.*

And with these agree Campbell, Lightfoot, Whitby, Poole, Olshausen, Meyer, Alford, and many other commentators and scholars. All those whom John baptized he buried beneath the waters, and raised them up again.

MUCH WATER NEEDED.

It is recorded that "John also was baptizing in Enon, near to Salim, because there was much water there." (John 3 : 23.) Why need much water, except for dipping, or burying the candidates in the act of baptism?

JOHN CALVIN, the great theologian, scholar, and commentator, whom Scaliger pronounced the most learned man in Europe, says: "From the words of John (chap. 3 : 23) it may be inferred that baptism was administered by John and Christ, by *plunging* the whole body under water." *Com. on John 3 : 23.*

POOLE says: "It is apparent that both Christ and John baptized by dipping the whole body in the water, else they need not have sought places where had been a great plenty of water." *Annot. John 3 : 23.*

WHITBY says: "Because there was much water there in which their whole bodies might be dipped." *Crit. Com. John 3 : 23.*

With these agree Bengel, Curcælleus, Adam Clarke, Geikie, Stanley, and others.

PHILIP AND THE EUNUCH.

"And they went down both into the water, both Philip and the eunuch, and he baptized him. And when they were come up out of the water, the Spirit of the Lord caught away Philip." (Acts 8 : 38.) Why go down into the water, both, or either of them, if not for an immersion?

VENEMA, the ecclesiastical historian, says: "It is without controversy, that baptism in the primitive church was administered by *immersion* into water, and not by sprinkling; seeing that John is said to have baptized in Jordan, and where there was much water, as Christ also did by his disciples in the neighborhood of those places. Philip also going down into the water baptized the eunuch." *Eccl. Hist., chap. I., sec. 138.*

To this may be added Calvin, Grotius,

Towerson, Poole, and others to the same effect.

THE TESTIMONY OF SCHOLARS.

Great men are not always wise. Our search should be for the *truth* wherever found; and though our final appeal in these matters is to the New Testament, still we are glad to use the testimony of distinguished scholars where it affirms the teachings of the Scriptures and confirms our position on the baptismal question. Especially so, as these scholars are not of our own, but of other denominations.

ZANCHIUS, the learned Roman Catholic Professor of Heidelberg, whose opinion De Courcy declared, "is worth a thousand others," said: "The proper signification of *baptize* is to *immerse*. plunge under, overwhelm in water." *Works, Vol. VI., p. 217. Geneva, 1619.*

LUTHER, the great German Reformer, says: "The term *baptism* is Greek; in Latin it may be translated *mersio;* since we *immerse* anything into water, that the whole may be covered with the water." *Works, Vol. I., p. 71. Wit. ed., 1582.*

MELANCTHON, the most scholarly and able

co-laborer with Luther, says: "Baptism is *immersion* into water, with this admirable benediction." *Melanc. Catec. Wit., 1580.*

CAVE, in his able work on Christian Antiquities, says: "The party to be baptized was *wholly immersed*, or put under water." *Prim. Christ., P. I. Chap. X. p. 320.*

BEZA, the learned translator of the New Testament, says: "Christ commanded us to be baptized, by which word it is certain *immersion* is signified." *Annot. on Mark 7 : 4.*

MEDE, the distinguished English scholar and divine, says: "There was no such thing as *sprinkling* used in the Apostles' days, nor for many ages after them." *Dis. on Titus 3 : 5.*

GROTIUS, whom his biographer calls one of the most illustrious names in literature, politics, and theology, says: "That baptism used to be performed by *immersion*, and not by pouring, appears by the proper signification of the word, and by the places chosen for the administration of the rite." *Annot. on Matt. 3 : 6; John 3 : 23.*

ADAM CLARK, the great Methodist commentator, says: "Alluding to the *immersions* practiced in the case of adults, wherein the person appeared to be *buried* under the water as Christ was buried in the heart of the earth." *Com. on Col. 2 : 12.*

FREDERICK MEYER, one of the ablest and most accurate exegetes of the present age, says: "*Immersion,* which the word in classic Greek and in the New Testament ever means." *Com. on Mark 7 : 4.*

DEAN ALFORD says: "The baptism was administered by the *immersion* of the whole person." *Greek Testament, Matt. 3 : 6.*

BISHOP BOSSUET, the celebrated French Catholic bishop, orator and counselor of state, says: "To baptize, signifies to *plunge,* as is granted by all the world." See *Stennett ad Russen, p. 174.*

DR. SCHAFF, the well-known church historian, says: "*Immersion,* and not sprinkling, was unquestionably the original form. This is shown by the very meaning of the words *baptizo, baptisma,* and *baptismos* used to designate the rite." *Hist. Apos. Ch., p. 488. Merc. ed., 1851. Also see Noel on Bap, Ch. 3, sec. 8.*

DEAN STANLEY, the distinguished scholar, and historian of the Oriental Church, says: "The practice of the Eastern Church, and the meaning of the word, leave no sufficient ground for question that the original form of baptism was *complete immersion* in the deep baptismal waters." *Hist. Eastern Church, p. 34.*

Prof. Fisher, of Yale College, the accomplished scholar and historian, says of the apostolic age: "The ordinary mode of baptism was by *immersion.*" *Hist. Christ. Church, p. 41.*

Prof. Riddle says: "There is no doubt that the usual mode of administering baptism in the early church, was by *immersion,* or plunging the whole body of the person baptized under water." *Christ. Antiq., p. 502.*

Add to the above the testimony of Bishops Taylor and Sherlock, Witsius, Poole, Vitringa, Diodati, Calvin, Samuel Clark, Bloomfield, Scholz, Neander, and many others to the same effect, none of whom were Baptists.

APOSTOLICAL ALLUSIONS.

What idea could the apostle have had as to the nature of baptism, when in two of his epistles he alludes to it as a *burial* except that it was a dipping or burial in water? To the Romans he says: "Therefore we are *buried* with him, by baptism, into death." (Rom. 6 : 4.) To the Colossians, in nearly the same language, "*Buried* with him in baptism." (Col. 2 : 12.) No one can misunderstand the meaning of these words. Neither sprinkling, pouring, washing, cleansing—nothing but a complete submersion—can represent a burial. And no candid mind could misunderstand such language, unless blinded or biased by prejudice, education, or sophistical reasoning from others.

ARCHBISHOP TILLOTSON makes this comment: "Anciently those who were baptized were *immersed* and *buried* in the water, to represent their death to sin; and then did rise up out of the water, to signify their entrance upon a new life. And to this custom the Apostle alludes." *Works, Vol. I. p. 179.*

JOHN WESLEY, the celebrated founder of Methodism, says: "Buried with him, alluding to the ancient manner of baptizing by *immersion*." *Note on Rom. 6 : 4.*

CONYBEARE says: "This passage cannot be understood unless it be borne in mind that the primitive baptism was by *immer-*

sion." *Life and Epist. St. Paul, Rom. 6 : 4.*

BLOOMFIELD says: "Here is a plain allusion to the ancient custom of baptizing by *immersion;* and I agree with Koppe and Rosenmüller, that there is reason to regret it should ever have been abandoned in most Christian churches; especially as it has so evident a reference to the mystical sense of baptism." *Recens. Synop., Rom. 6 : 4.*

WHITEFIELD says: "It is certain that in the words of our text (Rom. 6 : 4) there is an allusion to the manner of baptizing, which was by *immersion.*" *Eighteen Sermons, p. 297.*

MEYER says: "The candidate says to himself, now I enter into fellowship with the death of Christ; I am to be buried with Christ in the *immersion,* and in the *emersion* I rise with Christ to newness of life." *Com. on Rom. 6 : 4.*

Add to these the names of Bishop Fell, Dr. Doddridge, Adam Clark, Estius, Maldonatus, Fritsche, Benson, Diodati, Turretin, Zwingli, Whitby, Samuel Clarke, with others equally good in authority, and what no one ought to question seems to be put beyond doubt.

THE WITNESS OF HISTORY.

Learned and devout men have studied with care the early records of Christianity, and have written histories of the doctrines and customs of the churches, during the ages immediately succeeding the Apostles. What do they tell us as to the use of baptism during the first centuries after Christ?

BARNABAS, the companion of St. Paul, Hermas, writing about A. D. 95; Justin Martyr, about A. D. 140; Tertullian, about A. D. 204; Hippolytus, about A. D. 225; Gregory, about A. D. 360; Basil, about A. D. 360; Ambrose, about A. D. 374; Cyril, about A. D. 374; Chrysostom, about A. D. 400; all speak of being *dipped*, or *buried*, or *immersed*, or *plunged* in the water in baptism; and none of them make the least allusion to any application of water to the person for baptism, by sprinkling, pouring, washing, or any other mode whatever.

DR. WALL, whose learned and laborious researches in connection with his exhaustive work on the *History of Infant Baptism* left little for others to discover in this field of scholarship, says: "The Greek Church in all its branches does still use *immersion*, and so do all other Christians in the world, except the Latins. All those nations that do now, or formerly did submit to the Bishop of Rome, do ordinarily baptize their children by pouring or sprinkling. But *all other Christians in the world*, who never owned the Pope's usurped power, do and ever did *dip* their infants in the ordinary use. All the Christians in Asia, all in Africa, and about one-third in Europe are of the last sort." *Hist. Inf. Bap., Vol. II., p. 376. 3d ed.*

BINGHAM, in his *Origines*, the ablest work we have in English on Christian Antiquities, says: "The ancients thought that immersion, or *burying under water*, did more lively represent the death, burial, and resurrection of Christ, as well as our own death to sin and rising again unto righteousness." *Christ. Antiq., B. XI., Ch. XI.*

MOSHEIM says: "In this century (*the 1st*) baptism was administered in convenient places, without the public assemblies, and by *immersing* the candidate wholly in water." *Eccl. Hist. Cent. I., Part II., Ch. 4.*

NEANDER says: "In respect to the form of Baptism, it was in conformity to the original institution, and the original import of the symbol, performed by *immersion*, as a sign of entire baptism into the Holy Spirit, of being entirely penetrated with the same." *Ch. Hist., Vol. I., p. 310.* Also, *Plant. and Train., Vol. I., p. 222.*

SCHAFF says: "Finally, so far as it respects the mode and manner of outward baptizing, there can be no doubt that *immersion*, and not sprinkling, was the original normal form." *Hist. Christ. Ch., p. 488.*

PRESSENSÉ says: "Baptism, which was the sign of admission into the church, was administered by *immersion.* The convert was plunged beneath the water, and as he rose from it he received the laying on of hands." *Early Years of Christianity, p. 374.*

KURTZ says: "Baptism took place by a complete *immersion.*" *Church History, p. 41.*

KRAUS says: "Baptism was performed by *immersion* in the name of the Trinity." *Church History, p. 56. 1882.*

ELLICOTT says: "Jewish ablutions arrived at a ceremonial purity in the Levitical sense, and had nothing in common with the figurative act which portrayed through *immersion* the complete disappearance of the old nature, and by the *emerging* again the beginning of a totally new life." *Life of Christ, p. 110.*

FOR THIRTEEN CENTURIES.

It is proven that, not only was immersion practiced for baptism by Christ and his Apostles, but that for many ages after nothing else was known as baptism; and that for *thirteen hundred years* it was the common and prevailing form over the whole Christian world, with only exceptional departures, hereafter to be noticed. And that though the Latin or Roman Church did finally adopt sprinkling, claiming the right to change ordinances, the Greek and all the Oriental churches retained dipping, as they do to this day.

DR. STACKHOUSE says: "Several authors have shown and proved that this manner of *immersion* continued, as much as possible to be used for *thirteen hundred years* after Christ." *Hist. Bible, B. 8, Ch. 1.*

BISHOP BOSSUET says: "We are able to make it appear, by the acts of councils and by ancient rituals, that for *thirteen hundred years* baptism was thus administered [by immersion] throughout the whole church, as far as possible." *Cited, Stennet ad Russen p. 176.*

HAGENBACH says: "From the *thirteenth century* sprinkling came into more general use in the West. The Greek Church, however, and the church of Milan still retained the practice of *immersion.*" *Hist. Doct. Vol. II., p. 84, note 1.*

VAN OOSTERZEE, says: "This *sprinkling*, which appears to have first come generally into use in the *thirteenth century* in place of the entire *immersion* of the body, in imitation of the previous baptism of the sick, has certainly this imperfection, that the symbolical character of the act is expressed by it much less conspicuously than by complete immersion and burial under the water." *Christ. Dogmat., Vol. II., p. 749.*

COLEMAN says: "The practice of immersion continued even until the *thirteenth or fourteenth* century. Indeed, it has never been formally abandoned." *Anc. Christ. Exemp Ch. 19, Sec. 12.*

To the same effect is the testimony of Drs. Brenner, Von Cölln, Winer, Augusti, Bingham, and others.

AS TO THE GREEK CHURCH.

It is a notable fact, and worthy of record in this discussion, that the Greek Church has always retained immersion in baptism. This church extends over Greece, Russia, Arabia, Palestine, Abyssinia, Siberia, and other Oriental countries. Like the Latin Church, it has corrupted the primitive purity of gospel doctrine and practice with many absurd glosses and superstitious rites. It practices infant baptism, yet it is by *dipping*, even in the severe climate of Siberia; and it uses *trine* immersion, or dipping the candidate three times, once to each of the names in the sacred Trinity. But in all its branches immersion is retained.

THE EDINBURG ENCYCLOPEDIA says: "The Greek Church, as well as the Schismatics in the East, retained the custom of *immersing* the whole body; but the Western Church adopted, in the *thirteenth century*, the mode of sprinkling, which has been continued by the Protestants, Baptists only excepted." *Ency. Edin., Art. Baptism.*

These statements are fully confirmed by Stourdza, Ricaut, Deylingius, Buddeus, Wall, King, Broughton, Stanley, Coleman, and others, who have written on the state and history of the Greek Church.

THE DESIGN OF BAPTISM.

What was baptism intended to represent? As a religious rite it meant something, had some symbolic force, and represented some moral or spiritual fact or truth. Its meaning was clearly this: to show forth the death, burial, and resurrection of Christ, who died for our sins, and rose again for our justification. And every believer who receives this ordinance, professes thereby to have faith in the merits of Christ's death, as the ground of his own hope of salvation; to have fellowship also with his sufferings, and makes a declaration of his own death to sin, and rising to a new life in Christ. It also typifies the washing of regeneration; it further declares the candidate's hope of a resurrection from the dead, even as Christ, into the likeness of whose death he is buried, was raised up by the glory of the Father. Chiefly *death, burial,* and *resurrection;* the great facts of redemptive grace are by it set forth. Immersion in baptism does teach all this, and immersion alone can teach it. Careful students of the New

Testament have clearly seen this, and very generally confessed it, whatever may have been their practice.

BISHOP NEWTON says: "Baptism was usually performed by *immersion*, or dipping the whole body under water, to represent the death, burial, and resurrection of Christ, and thereby signify the person's own dying to sin, the destruction of its power, and his resurrection to a new life." *Pract. Expos. Cate., p. 297.*

BLOOMFIELD, Barnes, Schaff, Poole, Hammond, Barrows, Baxter, MacKnight, Olshausen, Grotius, Saurin, Buddeus, Pictetus, Frankius, Wall, Towerson, Adam Clark, Tyndale, and others, bear similar testimony as to the design of the ordinance, and how it is answered in immersion only.

A SUFFICIENCY OF WATER.

There have been found persons so ignorant, or so weak, or so perverse in their opposition to immersion, as to assert that the Jordan was a small stream, so nearly dry in the summer, that it had not sufficient depth of water for the immersion of the multitudes of the disciples of John and of Jesus said to have been baptized in it; and also that Jerusalem had no sufficient accommodation for the immersion of the thousands of converts at the Pentecost, and on subsequent occasions. People are becoming more intelligent, and more candid, and it is possible that such puerile objections are no more heard. But it may be well to give passing notice to the facts.

DR. EDWARD ROBINSON, at that time professor in the Union Theological Seminary, New York City, in 1840, made a careful survey of Palestine, including the Jordan valley and river. His published statements corroborate those of others previously made, as to the abundant supply of water, both in the Jordan, and in the city of Jerusalem. He cites the published statements of earlier explorers, whose works are known to the reading public. Seetzen, who visited that country in 1806; Burkhardt, who explored it in 1812; Irby and Mangles, in 1818; and Buckingham, who traveled through it about the same time. See *Robinson's Bib. Research, Vol. II. Sec. 10, pp 257–267.*

LIEUTENANT LYNCH, of the United States Navy, was, in 1848, sent out by our government in charge of an expedition to explore the river Jordan and the Dead Sea. Dr. Thomson, for a quarter of a century missionary in Syria and Palestine, traversed the land in 1857, and Dean Stanley in 1853, and others more recently. For a complete refutation of such puerile objections as those above mentioned, and a confirmation of Baptist claims, see the following works: Robinson's Biblical Researches, Vol. II. Sec. 10, pp. 257–267. Lynch's Dead Sea Expedition, Ch. 10 and 11. Thomson's The Land and the Book, Vol. II. pp. 445–6. Stanley's Syria and Palestine, Ch. 7, pp. 306–7. Barclay's The City of the Great Kings, Ch. 10. And other citations in "Baptist Church Directory."

THE RISE OF SPRINKLING.

The question will naturally arise, and very properly, when did sprinkling for baptism first come into use? And how came it to pass, that a human device superseded and took the place of a divine institution? These questions are fully and satisfactorily answered by Pedobaptist scholars themselves, whose testimony we accept as a justification of Baptist views.

For *two hundred and fifty years* after Christ we have no evidence of any departure from the primitive practice of immersion. At length the idea came to prevail that baptism possessed saving virtue, and had power to purify and sanctify the soul, making its salvation more secure. It was consequently thought unsafe to die unbaptized. Here was the germ of the pernicious dogma of "baptismal regeneration," the foundation alike of infant baptism, and of sprinkling instead of immersion.

The first authenticated instance of *sprinkling* occurred about the middle of the third century, or A. D. 250. This was the case of Novatian. The historian Eusebius gives this case, and Dr. Wall in his laborious researches could find no earlier instance; good evidence that no earlier existed. Novatian was dangerously sick, and believing himself about to die, was anxious to be baptized. The case seemed urgent, and as he was thought to be too feeble to be *immersed*, a substitute was resorted to, water was poured profusely over him as he lay in bed, so as to resemble as much as possible a submersion. The word used to describe this action (*perichutheis, perfusus*) has usually been rendered *besprinkle;* it rather means to pour profusely over and about one. This it was thought might answer the purpose in such an emergency.

From this time onward pouring and sprinkling were resorted to at times of extreme illness, or feebleness, where persons could not leave their beds, and hence was termed *clinic* baptism, from *clina,* a couch. But it was always regarded as a substitute for baptism, rather than baptism itself; and its validity was doubted. Novatian himself having recovered from his sickness, was objected to when his friends proposed to make him bishop, because, it was said, he had never been properly baptized. It was not, however, until the seventeenth century that sprinkling became common in Europe; in France first, and then extending through those countries over which the pope held sway. At length, accepted by Calvin and the Genevan Church, it extended into Scotland, by John Knox, and other Scotch refugees, who had found in Geneva a shelter from the persecution to which they had been exposed in their native country; then into England; and in 1643 it was adopted as the exclusive mode of baptism by a majority of one in the Westminster Assembly of Divines, and sanctioned by Parliament the next year. All of which is verified by Eusebius, Valesius, Wall, Salmasius, Venema, Taylor, Towerson, Grotius. "Ency. Brit."; "Edin. Ency." and other reliable historical authorities. [1]

---

[1] For more numerous citations on this subject, see the "Star Book on Christian Baptism," and "The Baptist Church Directory."

CHAPTER XI.

THE LORD'S SUPPER.

THE Lord's Supper, called also the "Eucharist," and the "Communion," is the most sacred act of Christian worship, and the highest expression of the mysteries of our holy religion. It is a service in which bread and wine—the *loaf* and the *cup*—are used to represent the body and the blood of Christ, the Lamb of God, slain for us. The bread is *broken*, distributed, and eaten; the wine is *poured*, distributed, and drunk by the members of the assembled church, to show the sacrifice of Christ, his body broken, and his blood shed for their redemption; and that by his death they have life. Being begotten of God through the operation of the Spirit, their new life is sustained and nourished by mystically feeding on him who is the Bread of God, which came down from heaven to give life to the world. He said: "This do in remembrance of me." "As oft as ye eat this bread and drink the cup ye proclaim the Lord's death, till he come." "Except ye eat the flesh of the Son of man, and drink his blood, ye have no life in you." "Whoso eateth my flesh and drinketh my blood, hath eternal life." "He that eateth my flesh, and drinketh my blood, dwelleth in me, and I in him." It is a divine reality, though a sublime mystery.

OPEN AND CLOSE COMMUNION.

The controversy between Baptists and other denominations, so far as the Lord's Supper is concerned, has no reference to its nature, the purpose for which it was instituted, the manner of its administration, or the effect of the elements on the participants. It has reference simply to the proper *subjects* for participation in the privilege. Who may, and who may not properly and of right come to the Lord's Table? On the question of what are the Scriptural qualifications of participants, Baptists and Pedobaptists differ—differ not as to the general rule to be applied, but as to its particular application. And this particular application leads to the controversy on what is called "*close communion,*" as practiced by Baptists, and to what is called "*open communion,*" as practiced by Pedobaptists.

What is open communion? *Open,* free or mixed communion is, strictly speaking, that which allows any one who desires, and believes himself qualified, to come to the Lord's Table, without any questions being asked, or conditions imposed by the church in which the ordinance is observed. But ordinarily the term is applied to the practice of the greater part of the Pedobaptist churches, which hold that *sprinkling* is lawful baptism, and invite, not all persons, but members of all evangelical churches, whatever be their view of church order and ordinances; holding them all as being baptized because they have been sprinkled.

What is close communion? *Close,* strict, or restricted communion is, properly speaking, that which does not invite all indiscriminately to the Lord's Table, but restricts the privilege to a particular class. But ordinarily the term is applied to the practice of Baptist churches, which invite only baptized believers, walking in orderly fellowship in their own churches. And by baptized believers, they mean, of course, immersed believers; not admitting sprinkling to be baptism at all.

ONE AND THE SAME RULE.

Observe further: That Baptists and Pedobaptists have one and the same rule in theory as to the proper qualification for participants, namely, they all hold that baptism is a prerequisite. That unbaptized persons have no legal right to the Lord's Supper, and cannot consistently be invited to it. Pedobaptists would not invite unbaptized persons to the Lord's Table, however good Christians, since such could not become church members, and the Supper is for those within the church, not for the outside world. For though a few churches and a few pastors, who in their extreme liberality might be disposed to invite everybody to the sacred ordinance, yet such a course would be contrary to their denominational standards, and opposed to the usages of their churches generally.

Further observe: They all practice a restriction, since they restrict the privilege to a particular class; namely, baptized believers, walking in orderly church fellowship. But Baptists and Pedobaptists differ as to what constitutes *baptism,* the one rejecting, and the other accepting the validity of sprinkling. Thus Baptists' custom is more "*close,*" and Pedobaptists' is more "*open,*" by the difference between their views of baptism; and by that difference only. *Therefore,* it is manifest that the question so called of "close" and "open" communion is really not a question of "communion" at all, but of what constitutes Scriptural baptism. Let that be settled, and the controversy as to the restriction of the Lord's Supper will cease.

THE BAPTIST POSITION.

Baptists hold that there are *three* imperative conditions precedent to the privileges of the Lord's Supper. 1. *Regeneration.* No unconverted person can with propriety, or of right, eat and drink at that sacred feast, in commemoration of Christ's death. They must be persons dead to sin, and alive to God; born again, through the operation of the Spirit. 2. *Baptism.* Buried with Christ in baptism on a profession of faith in him. No person, however good, and however manifestly regenerate, is prepared without baptism, according to the divine order, to receive the Supper. Without baptism he cannot enter the fellowship of the church, where the Supper alone is to be enjoyed. 3. *An orderly walk is necessary.* An upright and consistent Christian walk, and godly conversation among the saints, and before the world. For though one may be truly regenerate, and properly baptized, yet if he be a disorderly walker, violating his covenant obligations, living in sin, and bringing reproach on the Christian profession, he has no right to sit at the Lord's Table.

The ordinances are a sacred trust which Christ has committed to the churches as custodians, and which they are to watch and guard from all profane intrusion, and improper use, with the most sedulous fidelity. Baptists believe that in order to maintain the purity and spirituality of the churches, it is necessary to maintain the ordinances pure; and especially necessary to restrict the Supper to regenerate and godly persons, baptized on a profession of their faith, into the fellowship of the saints. To adopt any other rule, or to allow any larger liberty, would break down the distinction between the church and the world; would bring in a carnal and unconverted membership, and transfer the sacred mysteries of the body and the blood of Christ from the temple of God to the temple of Belial. This would be disloyalty to Christ.

The apostolic plan was as follows: Those who *believed* and *gladly received the word*, were *baptized*. Then they were *added to the church*. Then they continued steadfast in the *apostles' doctrine*, and fellowship, and in *breaking of bread*, and in *prayer*.

Notice, they were not baptized till they had received the word and believed. They were not added to the church till they had believed and been baptized. They did not engage in the breaking of bread (that is, the Supper), till they had believed, been baptized, and were added to the church. This is the divine order; and this is the order which Baptists maintain and defend.

PEDOBAPTIST CLOSE COMMUNION.

It has already been shown that Pedobaptists themselves practice a restricted or close communion, limiting the privilege to baptized (as they call them) members of evangelical churches, and that their communion is more liberal than that of the Baptists only, and only by so much as their baptism (so-called) is more liberal than that of Baptists.

But in some respects Pedobaptists practice a "close communion," restrictive in its conditions, far beyond anything known to Baptists whose illiberality they are accustomed to magnify. They exclude a large class of their own members from the Lord's Table—namely, *baptized children!* Baptists do not deny the Lord's Supper to their own members in good standing. If children are suitable subjects for baptism, it seems most unreasonable and unjust to deny them the Supper. If they can be benefited by one ordinance, can they not be equally benefited by the other? If they can receive the one on the faith of sponsors, can they not receive the other in the same way? Who has authorized parents or ministers to give baptism to unconverted and unconscious children, and refuse them the Lord's Supper? By denying the Supper to baptized children, Pedobaptists act contrary to the traditions of the ancient churches, which they are accustomed to cite with so much assurance, in defense of infant baptism. Do they not know that those ancient churches (not the primitive churches) gave the Lord's Supper to infants for many centuries? And the Greek Church, through all its branches, continues still the same practice.

Dr. Coleman says: "After the general introduction of infant baptism, in the *second and third centuries*, the sacrament continued to be administered to all who had been baptized, whether infants or adults. The reason alleged by Cyprian and others for this practice was, that age was no impediment. Augustine strongly advocates the practice. The custom continued for several centuries. It is mentioned in the third Council of Tours, A. D. 813; and even the Council of Trent, A. D. 1545, only decreed that it should not be considered essential to salvation. It is still scrupulously observed by the Greek Church." *Anc. Christ. Exemp., Ch. 22, Sec. 8; Bing. Orig., B. 15, Ch. 4, Sec. 7. Many other writers bear the same testimony.*

THE POWER OF SYMPATHY.

There is a small class of Baptists who are at times inclined to desire, and it may be, to seek a wider liberty at the Lord's Table than they find accorded in their own churches. The one prevailing argument with them is *sympathy*. To them it seems kindly and fraternal to invite all who say they love our common Lord and Saviour to unite in commemorating his death in the Supper. Even if they have not been baptized, they themselves believe they have, and they are good Christian people. "Why stand upon a technicality?" they say. To such the service is merely a sentimental service; a kind of love feast to show Christian fellowship, rather than an instituted commemoration of their dying Lord. They have neither Scripture, logic, expediency, the scholarship, nor the concurrent practice of Christendom, either past or present, to sustain their position. But *sympathy* influences them; yet sympathy should not control conduct in matters of faith, or in acts of conscience. It is a grave perversion when affection for his disciples sways us more than fidelity to our Lord. We should not be so kind to *them* as to be untrue to *him*. Sincere Christians will honor those who are loyal to Christ, even though they differ in opinion.

THREE FACTS EXPLAINED.

Baptists give the following reasons in justification of their course in the following cases:

1. They do not invite Pedobaptists to the Lord's Supper with them, because such persons are not baptized, as has been shown, they being simply sprinkled. They may be true converts, and have the spiritual qualifications, but they are destitute of the ceremonial qualification—baptism. The "buried in baptism" comes before the "breaking of bread."

2. They do not accept the invitation of Pedobaptist churches to eat at the Lord's Table with them, for the same reason; they are not baptized Christians. And while they appreciate their Christian fellowship, they could not accept their church fellowship, and sit at the Lord's Table with them, without accepting their sprinkling and indorsing their baptismal errors.

3. They do not invite immersed members of Pedobaptist churches to the Lord's Supper with them, because such persons, though they may be truly regenerate and properly baptized, are walking disorderly by remaining in and giving countenance to churches which

hold and practice serious errors as to both the ordinances. These churches use sprinkling for baptism and administer the ordinance to infants, both of which are unscriptural. And yet such persons, by remaining in them, encourage and support these errors, instead of protesting against them by leaving them. They insist on immersion for themselves, and yet by a strange inconsistency give their fellowship and influence to perpetuate and sanction sprinkling for others. This is inconsistent and disorderly Christian walking; and, therefore, very properly, Baptists decline to invite them to the Lord's Supper.

PEDOBAPTIST WITNESSES.

In further proof that the position of Baptists as to the Lord's Supper is correct and Scriptural; that the difficulty lies with baptism, and not with the Supper; and that they must still continue to restrict the ordinance to baptized believers, or else admit that sprinkling is baptism, we cite the concessions of distinguished Pedobaptist scholars and divines in evidence on our side.

JUSTIN MARTYR, one of the early Christian Fathers, says of the Supper: "This food is called by us the Eucharist, of which it is not lawful for any one to partake but such as believe the things taught by us to be true, and have been baptized." *Apol. I. C. 65, 66. See Schaff's Church Hist. Ch. 2, p. 516.*

MOSHEIM, in his Church History, says: "Neither those doing penance, nor those not yet baptized, were allowed to be present at the celebration of this ordinance." *Eccl. Hist., Cent. 3, Part 2, Ch. 4, Sec. 3.*

NEANDER, the great Church historian, says: "At this celebration, as may be easily concluded, no one could be present who was not a member of the Christian Church, and incorporated into it by the rite of baptism." *Ch. Hist., Vol. I., 327. Boston, 1849.*

CAVE, one of the ablest writers on Christian Antiquities, says the participants in the primitive church were those "that had embraced the doctrine of the gospel, and had been baptized into the faith of Christ. For, looking upon the Lord's Supper as the highest and most solemn act of religion, they thought they could never take care enough in the dispensing of it." *Prim. Christ, Part I., Ch. 11, p. 333.*

BINGHAM, in his able work on the Antiquities of the Christian Church, says of the early Christians: "As soon as a man was baptized he was communicated"—that is, admitted to the communion. Baptism, therefore, essentially preceded the Supper. —*Christ Antiq. B. 12, Ch. 4, Sec. 9, B. 15, Ch. 3.*

DR. WALL, who searched the records of antiquity for facts illustrating the history of the ordinances, says: "No church ever gave the communion to any persons before they were baptized. Among all the absurdities that were ever held, none ever maintained that any person should partake of the communion before he was baptized." *Hist. Inf. Bap., Part II., Ch. 9.*

DR. COLEMAN says of the early churches: "None indeed but believers in full communion with the church were permitted to be present." "But agreeably to all the laws and customs of the church, baptism constituted membership with the church. All baptized persons were legitimately numbered among the communicants as members of the church." *Anc. Christ. Exemp., Ch. 21 Sec. 8.*

DR. SCHAFF says: "The communion was

a regular part, and, in fact, the most important and solemn part of the Sunday worship, ... in which none but full members of the church could engage." *Ch. Hist., Vol. I., p. 392. New York, 1871.*

DR. DODDRIDGE says: "It is certain that so far as our knowledge of primitive antiquity reaches, no unbaptized person received the Lord's Supper." *Lectures, pp. 511, 512.*

DR. DICK says: "An uncircumcised man was not permitted to eat the Passover; and an unbaptized man should not be permitted to partake of the Eucharist." *Theol., Vol. II., p. 220.*

DR. BAXTER says: "What man dares go in a way which hath neither precept nor example to warrant it, from a way that hath full current of both? Yet they that will admit members into the visible church without baptism do so." *Plain Scripture Proof, p. 24.*

DR. DWIGHT, President of Yale College, and author of "Systematic Theology," says: "It is an indispensable qualification for this ordinance that the candidate for communion be a member of the visible church in full standing. By this, I intend that he should be a man of piety; that he should have made a public profession of religion, and that he should have been baptized." *Syst. Theol., Ser. 160, B. 8, Ch. 4, Sec. 7.*

DR. GRIFFIN, one of the fathers of New England Congregationalism, says: "I agree with the advocates of close communion in two points: 1. That baptism is the initiatory ordinance which introduces us into the visible church; of course, where there is no baptism, there are no visible churches. 2. That we ought not to commune with those who are not baptized, and of course not church members, even if we regard them as Christians." *Letter on Baptism, 1829, cited by Curtis on Com., p. 125.*

DR. HIBBARD, a leading Methodist scholar and divine, says: "In one principle Baptist and Pedobaptist churches agree. They both agree in rejecting from communion at the table of the Lord, and in denying the rights of church fellowship to all who have not been baptized." And with admirable frankness, he adds: "The charge of *close communion* is no more applicable to the Baptists than to us [Pedobaptists]; insomuch as the question of church fellowship with them is determined by as liberal principles as it is with any other Protestant churches, so far, I mean, as the present subject is concerned—i. e., *it is determined by valid baptism.*" *Hibbard on Christ. Bap., P. II., p. 174.*

DR. BULLOCK, another Methodist divine, says: "Close communion, as it is generally termed, is the only logical and consistent course for Baptist churches to pursue. If their premises are right, their conclusion is surely just as it should be." And he commends the firmness of Baptists in not inviting to the communion those whom they regard as unbaptized. He says: "They do not feel willing to countenance such laxity in Christian discipline. Let us honor them for their steadfastness in maintaining what they believe to be a Bible precept, rather than criticise and censure because they differ with us concerning the intent and mode of Christian baptism, and believe it to be an irrepealable condition of coming to the Lord's table." *What Christians Believe.*

THE INDEPENDENT, one of the most widely circulated, and perhaps the most influential Pedobaptist paper in the country, in an editorial, says: "Leading writers of all denominations declare that converts must be baptized before they can be invited to the communion table. This is the position generally taken. But Baptists regarding sprinkling as a nullity—no baptism at all—look upon Presbyterians, Methodists, and others, as unbaptized persons." "The other churches cannot urge the Baptists to become open communionists till they themselves take the position that all who love our Lord Jesus Christ, the unbaptized as well as the baptized, may be invited to the communion table." *Editorial, July, 1879.*

THE CONGREGATIONALIST, the organ of the New England Congregational Churches, in an editorial, says: "Congregationalists have uniformly, until here and there an exception has arisen of late years, required baptism and church membership as the prerequisite of a seat at the table of the Lord. It is a part of the false 'liberality' which now prevails in certain quarters, to welcome everybody 'who thinks he loves Christ' to commune in his body and blood. Such a course is the first step in breaking down that distinction between the church and the world, which our Saviour emphasized; and it seems to us it is an unwise and mistaken act for which no Scriptural warrant exists." *Editorial, July 9, 1879.*

THE OBSERVER, of New York, the oldest and leading Presbyterian journal of this country, said: "It is not a want of charity which compels the Baptist to restrict his invitation. He has no hesitation in admitting the personal piety of his unimmersed brethren. Presbyterians do not invite the unbaptized, however pious they may be. It is not uncharitable. It is not bigotry on the part of Baptists to confine their communion to those whom they consider the baptized."

THE INTERIOR, of Chicago, the organ of Western Presbyterians, said: "The difference between our Baptist brethren and ourselves is an important difference. We agree with them, however, in saying that unbaptized persons should not partake of the Lord's Supper. Their view compels them to think that we are not baptized, and shuts them up to close communion. Close communion is, in our judgment, a more defensible position than open communion, which is justified on the ground that baptism is not a prerequisite to the Lord's Supper. To charge Baptists with bigotry because they abide by the logical consequences of their system is absurd."

THE CHRISTIAN ADVOCATE, of New York, the leading journal of American Methodists, said: "The regular Baptist churches in the United States may be considered to-day as practically a unit on *three points*—the non-use of infant baptism, the immersion of believers only upon a profession of faith, and the administration of the holy communion to such only as have been immersed by ministers holding these views. In our opinion the Baptist Church owes its amazing prosperity largely to its adherence to these views. In doctrine and government, and in other respects, it is the same as the Congregationalists. In numbers, the regular Baptists are more than six times as great as the Congregationalists. It is not bigotry to adhere to one's convictions, providing the spirit of Christian love prevails."

THE EPISCOPAL RECORDER said: "The close communion of the Baptist churches is but the necessary sequence of the fundamental idea out of which their existence has grown. No Christian Church would willingly receive to its communion even the humblest and truest believer in Christ who had not been baptized. With Baptists, immersion only is baptism, and they therefore of necessity exclude from the Lord's Table all who have not been immersed. It is an essential part of the system—the legitimate carrying out of the creed."

CHAPTER XII.

INFANT BAPTISM.

ONE of the customs held and upheld by Pedobaptist churches, which Baptists seriously condemn, is infant baptism. It is practiced by both Roman Catholics and Protestants as a religious institution; and though not held as sacredly, or practiced as widely as formerly, it still prevails to a wide extent throughout the Christian world. And yet it was not instituted by Christ, nor practiced by his apostles, nor known in the primitive churches, and has neither sanction nor recognition in the word of God. It is for this reason that Baptists utterly reject and condemn the custom, as not simply useless and without authority, but as a most pernicious and hurtful usage; that it is injurious both to the child that receives it, and to the church which allows it, can be easily shown. Baptism before faith, and without a profession of it, contradicts and does violence to all New Testament teaching.

NOT OF SCRIPTURAL AUTHORITY.

Now, that infant baptism is not of Scriptural authority, and was not known in the first Christian ages, nearly all its advocates and defenders have with considerable candor admitted. Only a few of their historians and scholars can be cited here.

DR. WILLIAM WALL, a learned divine of the English Church, who wrote the History of Infant Baptism, a work so able that the clergy in convocation assembled gave him a vote of thanks for his defense of the custom, says: "Among all the persons that are recorded as baptized by the Apostles, there is no express mention of any infants." *Hist. Inf. Bap., Intro., pp. 1, 55.*

THOMAS FULLER, the historian, says: "We do freely confess there is neither express precepts nor precedent in the New Testament for the Baptism of Infants." *Infants' Advoc., pp. 71, 150.*

LUTHER says: "It cannot be proved by the sacred Scriptures that infant baptism was instituted by Christ, or begun by the first

Christians after the Apostles. *Vanity of Inf. Bap., Part II., p. 8.*

NEANDER says: "Baptism was administered at first only to adults, as men were accustomed to conceive of *baptism* and *faith* as strictly connected. We have all reason for not deriving infant baptism from apostolic institution." *Ch. Hist., Vol. I., p. 311; Plant. and. Train, Vol. I., p. 222.*

PROF. LANGE says: "All attempts to make out infant baptism from the New Testament fail. It is totally opposed to the spirit of the apostolic age, and to the fundamental principles of the New Testament." *Inf. Baptism, p. 101.*

PROF. JACOBI says: "Infant baptism was established neither by Christ, nor by the Apostles." *Art. Bap. Kitto's Cycl. Bib. Lit.*

DR. HANNA says: "Scripture knows nothing of the baptism of infants." *North Brit. Review. Aug., 1852.*

PROF. HAGENBACH says: "The passages from Scripture cited in favor of infant baptism as a usage of the primitive church are doubtful, and prove nothing." *Hist. Doct., pp. 190, 193.*

BISHOP BURNETT, Baxter, Goodwin,

Limborch, Celarius, Field, and many others bear similar testimony.

WHEN DID IT RISE?

Since the New Testament knows nothing of infant baptism, and since it was neither instituted by Christ, nor practiced by his Apostles, what was its origin, and when did it come into use?

TERTULLIAN is the first who mentions the custom, and he opposes it. This was at the close of the second century, or about A. D. 200. His opposition to it proves two things: *First*, that it was in occasional use, at least. *Second*, that it was of recent origin, since had it been long used some earlier record of it could be found. *Neander, Ch. Hist., Vol. I., p. 311.*

BINGHAM could find no earlier allusion to it than that of Tertullian, though he believed it arose earlier. It must, therefore, as is generally agreed, have had its origin about the beginning of the *third century.*

CURCELLÆUS says: "The baptism of infants in the *two first* centuries after Christ was altogether unknown; but in the *third* and *fourth* was allowed by some few. In the *fifth* and following ages it was generally received." *Inst. Christ. Religion, B. I., Ch. 12.*

SALMASIUS says: "In the *first two* centuries no one was baptized, except, being instructed in the faith and acquainted with the doctrines of Christ, he was able to profess himself a believer." *Hist. Bapt. Suicer. Thesaur., Vol. II., p. 1136.*

Such testimony is conclusive, and quite sufficient, though much more of a similar character might be added.

But observe: That when the baptism of children began, it was not that of unconscious infants at all, as is now practiced, but, as Bunsen declares, of "little growing children, from six to ten years old." And he asserts that Tertullian "does not say one word of new-born infants." Cyprian, an African bishop, at the close of the *third* century, urged the baptism of infants proper, because of the saving efficacy of the ordinance; and he is called the inventor, or father, of infant baptism. *Bunsen's Hippol. and His Age, Vol. III., pp. 192–5.*

WHY DID IT RISE?

There is even less difficulty in tracing the cause than in finding the origin of infant baptism. It originated in a perversion of Christian doctrine, and was itself the perversion of a Christian ordinance.

All students of ecclesiastical history know that at an early period corruptions perverted Christian faith and practice. Among these, one of the earliest was that of an undue efficacy attributed to baptism. Its sanctity was so exalted that it was believed to have power to wash away sins, and cleanse the soul for heaven. By it the sick were supposed to be prepared for death, and salvation made more certain by its efficacy. Anxious parents therefore desired their dying children to be thus prepared—"washed in the laver of regeneration," as it was termed—that they might be sure of salvation. And here came in that pernicious error of "baptismal regeneration," which gave rise to infant baptism, and which has through all these ages clung with more or less pertinacity to the clergy and laity of all churches which have practiced it.

SALMASIUS says: "An opinion prevailed that no one could be saved without being baptized; and for that reason the custom arose of baptizing infants." *Epist. Jus.*

Pac. See Booth's Pedo. Exam., Ch. III., Sec. 3.

VENEMA declares that "the ancients connected a regenerating power with baptism." He cites Justin Martyr, Irenæus, Clemens, Tertullian, and Cyprian as holding that opinion. *Eccl. Hist., Vol. 4, p. 3, Secs. 2, 3, 4.*

CHRYSOSTOM, writing about A. D. 398, as cited by Suicerus, says: "It is impossible without baptism to obtain the kingdom," and as cited by Wall he says: "If sudden death seize us before we are baptized, though we have a thousand good qualities, there is nothing to be expected but hell." *Suicer., Thesaur. Eccl., Vol. I., p. 3.*

WADDINGTON, in his Church History, says, in reference to the *third* century: "A belief was gaining ground among the converts, and was inculcated among the heathen, that the act of baptism gave remission of all sins committed previously." *Hist. of Church, Ch. II., p. 53.*

PROF. FISHER says: "Very early baptism was so far identified with regeneration as to be designated by that term. This rite was considered essential to salvation. A virtue was believed to reside in the baptismal water itself." *Hist. Christ. Ch., p. 83.*

Do its advocates and supporters hold the same view now? Do parents and ministers still believe that the baptism of unconscious infants secures, or makes more sure, their salvation? If not, why do they practice it?

PROF. LANGE'S words are weighty, and should be carefully pondered by Protestant defenders of this Papal emanation. He says: "Would the Protestant Church fulfill and attain to its final destiny, the baptism of new-born children must of necessity be abolished. It has sunk down to a mere formality, without any meaning for the child." *History of Protestantism, p. 34.*

Many good people, familiar with infant baptism and surrounded by its influences, have naturally learned to reverence it as of divine appointment, and some of them really believe it is taught or sanctioned by the New Testament. But Baptists are right in rejecting it as something utterly without foundation in the word of God.

HOUSEHOLD BAPTISMS.

Much stress is laid by some of the advocates of infant baptism on the fact that in the Acts of the apostles several cases of household baptism are mentioned. And it is asked with an air of assurance: "If entire households were baptized, must there not have been children among them? And were they not baptized also?" To this it is sufficient to reply, that nothing is said of children, and we have no right to put into the Scriptures what we do not find in them. All inference that such households contained infants, and that such infants were baptized, is the purest fiction in the world. If Christian institutions could be built on so slight a foundation as that, we could bring in all the mummeries of the Greek or the Roman Church, and all the ceremonies of the Mosaic ritual.

One thing is certain: if in those households any children were baptized, they were old enough to receive the gospel and to believe on Christ, and were thus suitable subjects for the ordinance, and for church fellowship. For it is said, "*They believed, and gladly received the word.*" There are thousands of Baptist churches into whose fellowship whole households have been baptized—parents and children, and perhaps others connected with them. But all were old enough to *believe* and to make *profession* of their faith. So evidently it was in these households.

The more prominent of these households are that of Lydia, mentioned in Acts 16; that of the Philippian jailer, mentioned also in Acts 16; and that of Stephanas, mentioned in 1 Cor. 1. Now note what a few distinguished Pedobaptist scholars say of these cases.

DR. NEANDER says: "We cannot prove that the Apostles ordained infant baptism; from those places where the baptism of a whole family is mentioned, we can draw no such conclusion." *Planting and Training, p. 162, N. Y. Ed., 1865.*

PROF. JACOBI says: "In none of these instances has it been proved that there were little children among them." *Kitto's Bib. Cyc., Art. Bap.*

DR. MEYER says: "That the baptism of children was not in use at that time appears evident from 1 Cor. 7: 14." *Comment. on Acts 16: 15.*

DR. DE WETTE says: "This passage has been adduced in proof of the apostolical authority of infant baptism; but there is no proof here that any except adults were baptized." *Com. New Test., Acts 16: 15.*

DR. OLSHAUSEN says: "There is altogether wanting any conclusive proof text for the baptism of infants in the age of the Apostles." *Com. on Acts 16: 15.*

BISHOP BLOOMFIELD says of the jailer: "It is taken for granted that his family became Christians as well as himself." *Com. on Acts 16: 31.*

CALVIN, Doddridge, Henry, and other commentators declare that in this case the household all believed, and therefore were baptized and did rejoice. MacKnight considers the case of the household of Stephanas as giving no countenance to the baptism of infants. And with him agree Guise, Hammond, Doddridge, and others.

As to the argument used by some, that baptism came in the place of circumcision, it is too weak and puerile, too far fetched and destitute of reason, to claim the serious regard of intelligent and candid minds.

CHAPTER XIII.

CHURCH GOVERNMENT.

A CHRISTIAN church is a society with a corporate life, organized on some definite plan, adapted to some definite purpose, which it proposes to accomplish. It has, therefore, its officers and ordinances, its laws and regulations, fitted to administer its government and carry out its purposes. The question then arises, What is the true and proper form of church organization and government? We do not care to inquire as to the various and contradictory forms, as we see them about us in the different denominations, but what was the organic form and government of the first churches, planted by and moulded under the hands of Christ's inspired apostles.

There are *three* special and widely different forms of church government which have gained prevalence in Christian communities during past ages, and which are still maintained with varied success, each of which claims to have been the original primitive form :

1. The *prelatical,* in which the governing power resides in prelates, or diocesan bishops, and the higher clergy; as in the Roman, Greek, English, and most Oriental churches.

2. The *presbyterian,* in which the governing power resides in assemblies, synods, presbyteries, and sessions; as in the Scottish Kirk, the Lutheran, and the various Presbyterian churches.

3. The *independent,* in which the body is self-governing, each single and local church administering its own government by the voice of the majority of its members; as among Baptists, Congregationalists, Independents, and some other bodies.

Now which of these modes of church life and administration is taught in the New Testament, if either? or which best accords with the constitution and government of the apostolic churches?

Baptists hold that each separate, local church is an independent body, governing itself according to the laws of Christ, as found in the New Testament. That each such church is independent of all other churches, and of all other persons, so far as administration is concerned, owing comity and fellowship to all, but allegiance and submission to none. The government is administered by the body of the members, where no one possesses a pre-eminence of authority, but each enjoys an equality of rights, and in which, in matters of opinion, the majority decides.

That this style of church structure is according to the New Testament appears evident from a study of the sacred records themselves. The apostles treated the churches as independent bodies. Their epistles were addressed to the churches as such; they reported their doings to them; enjoined upon them the duty of discipline; exhorted, instructed, and reproved them as independent and responsible bodies. They recognized the right of the churches to elect their own teachers and officers, a primary and fundamental right, which, when conceded, supposes all other rights and powers necessary to a self-governing community acting under divinely given laws.

NEANDER, the distinguished historian, says of the first age: "The churches were taught to govern themselves." "The brethren chose their own officers from among themselves." "In respect to the election of church officers, the ancient principle was still adhered to: that the consent of the community was necessary to the validity of every such election, and each one was at liberty to offer reasons against it." *Introd. Coleman's Prim. Christ'y, p 19; Ch. Hist., Vol. I., p. 199; Plant. and Train., p. 156.*

MOSHEIM says of the first century: "In those primitive times, each Christian Church was composed of the *people*, the presiding *officers*, and the assistants, or *deacons*. These must be the component parts of every society. The principal voice was that of the *people*, or of the whole body of Christians." "The assembled people, therefore, elected their own rulers and teachers." Of the second century, he adds: "One president, or bishop, presides over each church. He was created by the common suffrages of the people." "During a great part of this century, all the churches continued to be, as at first, *independent* of each other. Each church was a kind of small, independent republic, governing itself by its own laws, enacted, or at least sanctioned, by the people." *Eccl.*

Hist., Cent. 1, Part 1, Ch. 2, Sec. 5, 6; Cent. 2, Ch. 2, Sec. 1, 2.

COLEMAN says: "These churches, where ever formed, became separate and independent bodies, competent to appoint their own officers and administer their own government without reference or subordination to any control, authority, or foreign power. No fact connected with the history of the primitive church is more fully established or more generally conceded." *Prim. Christ. Exempt., Ch. 4, Sec. 4, p. 95.*

ARCHBISHOP WHATELY, Dr. Barrow, Dr. Burton, Dr. Waddington,—all of them Church of England divines,—fully agree with this testimony, and confirm the evidence cited.

GEISELER, the historian, says, concerning early changes: "Country churches, which had grown up around some city, seem, with their bishops, to have been usually, in a certain degree, under the authority of the mother church. With this exception, all the churches were alike independent, though some were especially held in honor, on such grounds as their apostolic origin, or the importance of the city in which they were situated." *Period 1, Div. 1, Ch. 3, Sec. 52.*

situated." Period 1, Div. 1, Ch. 3, Sec. 52.

Further discussion on this subject is not needed. The point is proven, and the independent form of church government is manifestly primitive and apostolic, as advocated and practiced by Baptists.

CHAPTER XIV.

CHURCH OFFICERS.

How many, and what are the Scriptural officers of a Christian church? For a church, being a society, must have not only laws, but officers to execute them. How many orders are there in the ministry? These are questions which have at times greatly divided the Christian world.

Baptists assert that the officers of a church are *two*,—and of right, can be no more,—*pastor* and *deacons*. In this opinion agree some other denominations, while the various Episcopal sects insist that there should be three sects—*deacons*, *priests*, and *bishops*, to which the Church of England adds archbishops. Others add to this number indefinitely; and the Romish Church carries the list up to ten or twelve, ending with the pope. Now it is not so much what this church teaches or practices, but on what basis were the primitive churches — the churches of inspiration—organized. Our Lord did not live to shape, and model, and put in order all things for the full equipment of his people, that they might be thoroughly furnished unto all good works, but he did give to his apostles a spirit of wisdom by which they should be able to do all this, and carry out his plans, in the organization of his kingdom after he had left them. We assume that the first churches were organized on the divine plan, and seek to ascertain what that plan was.

In the New Testament, the words *bishop*, *presbyter*, *elder* are used to designate church officers. They all, however, designate the same office, and therefore officially mean the same thing; indeed, they are not unfrequently applied to the same individual. The bishop—called also presbyter, or elder—was the *pastor*, or overseer of the spiritual flock, watching, guiding, and feeding it, as the shepherd does his sheep. The *deacons* were chosen to attend to the temporal interests of the church, as appears by the election of the seven, recorded in the sixth chapter of Acts. This was done in order that the apostles might be free from the temporal cares, and thus able to give their attention more exclusively to the spiritual welfare of the people. The word *deacon* means a *minister*, a *servant*. It is sometimes applied to the apostles, and even to Christ himself, in that general sense as one who "came, not to be ministered unto, but to minister, and to give his life a ransom for many." Some of the first deacons were also efficient preachers of the gospel, but their work as deacons pertained to other service in the churches. While, therefore, the deacon is a church officer, his office does not constitute an order in the ministry at all, its functions belonging to temporal concerns, and not to a spiritual service. The service usually performed by clerks, trustees, and the like, it may be presumed, so far as such service was needed in the first churches, was devolved on the deacons.

Pastors, by whatever name they may have been known, had the same service, and were of the same grade, dignity, and authority. In the first churches there were no high orders of clergy placed over lower grades, and over the churches ruling with superior authority. All were equals among equals, and all equally ministered to the churches. If in the same church there might chance to be several to whom the titles *bishop*, *presbyter*, or *elder* were applied, they were all of equal rank or authority, though one might be selected to serve as the pastor of the church, and devote himself to its local interests; while the others might give themselves to more general missionary work.

NEANDER says: "The word *presbyter*, or *elder*, indicates rather the dignity of the office, since presbyters among the Jews were usually aged and venerable; while *bishop*, or *episcopos*, designated the nature of their work as overseers, or pastors of the churches. The former title was used by Jewish Christians as a name familiar in the synagogue; while the latter was chiefly used by the Greek and other Gentile converts, as more familiar and expressive to them." "They were not designed to exercise absolute authority, but to act as presiding officers and guides of an ecclesiastical republic: to conduct all things, with the co-operation of the communities, as their ministers, and not as their masters." *Introd. to Cole. Prim. Ch., p. 20; Ch. Hist. Vol. 1., p. 184; Plant. and Train., p. 147.*

MOSHEIM says: "The rulers of the

churches were denominated sometimes *presbyters*, or *elders*, a designation borrowed from the Jews, and indicative rather of the wisdom than the age of the persons, and sometimes also *bishops;* for it is most manifest that both terms are promiscuously used in the New Testament of one and the same class of persons." "In these primitive times, each Christian church was composed of the *people*, the presiding *officers*, and the assistants, or *deacons*. These must be the components of every society." *Eccl. Hist., Cent. 1, p. 2; Ch., 2, Secs. 5, 8.*

GIESELER asserts: "The new churches everywhere formed themselves on the model of the mother church at Jerusalem. At the head of each were the *elders* (*presbyter, bishop*), all officially of equal rank, though in several instances a peculiar authority seems to have been conceded to some one individual from personal considerations." *Ch. Hist., Part 1, Div. 1, Ch. 2, Sec. 29.*

WADDINGTON declares: "It is also true that in the earliest government of the first Christian society,—that of Jerusalem,—not the *elders* only, but the 'whole church,' were associated with the apostles; and it is even certain that the terms *bishop* and *elder*, or *presbyter*, were in the first instance and for a short period, sometime used synonymously, and indiscriminately applied to the same order in the ministry." *Hist. Christ. Church, Ch. 2, Sec. 2.*

ARCHBISHOP USHER says that "*bishop* and *presbyter* differed only in degree, and not in order." See *Cole. Anc. Christ. Exemp., Ch. 8, Sec. 6.*

BISHOP BURNETT says: "As for the notion of distinct offices of *bishop* and *presbyter*, I confess it is not so clear to me." *Vindic. Ch. of Sects. p. 366.*

DR. COLEMAN says: "It is generally admitted by Episcopal writers on this subject, that in the New Testament, and in the earliest ecclesiastical writings, the terms *bishops* and *presbyters*, or elders, are synonymous, and denote one and the same office." "The office of *presbyter* was undeniably identical with that of *bishop*, as has been shown above." "Only *two orders* of officers are known in the church until the close of the second century. Those of the first are styled either *bishops* or *presbyters*; of the second, *deacons*." *Anc. Christ. Exemp., Ch. 8, Sec. 6; Ch. 6, Sec. 5.*

This author cites many of the early Christian Fathers who bore the same testimony, among whom are Clement of Rome, Polycarp, Justin Martyr, Irenæus, Jerome, Chrysostom, Theodoret, and others. Many prelatical writers, besides these above quoted, frankly admit the same facts.

The Apostle Paul, it is stated (Acts 20 : 17, 18), called together the *elders* (*presbyters*) of the Ephesian Church. But in verse 28 he calls these officers *overseers* (*episcopous*). Here the terms *presbuteros* and *episcopos* were certainly used interchangeably.

Paul and Timothy, in their address to the Philippian Christians, specify three classes as evidently constituting the entire body of disciples. They say: "To all the *saints* in Christ Jesus, which are at Philippi, with the *bishops* and *deacons*." Saints, bishops, and deacons embraced the whole church.

Timothy was instructed by Paul as to the qualifications of pastors to be placed over the churches. (1 Tim. 3 : 1.) Particular directions are given as to both *bishops* and *deacons*, but no mention is made of elders—clearly because they were the same as bishops.

Titus is likewise enjoined to secure pastors for the church in Crete. (Titus 1 : 5, 7.) These pastors are called *elders* in verse 5 and *bishops* in verse 7.

Pastors and *deacons*, therefore, are two orders, and these officers simply were known or needed in the apostolic churches. In this, also, the views held by Baptists are in harmony with the customs of the churches in the first and purest age of Christian history.

CHAPTER XV.

BAPTIST HISTORY.

It is sometimes asked: "When and where did the Baptists originate? Who were their founders? What is their history?" These are questions of interest; but a more important one would be: "Are they right? Is their faith according to the teachings of the New Testament?" Many things which are old are not true. Creeds and sects may boast a venerable antiquity, while the word of God utterly condemns them. Any organization that cannot reasonably claim Christ for its founder has small right to the name of a Christian church, no matter how old it may be.

Baptists claim to be built on the foundation of the apostles and prophets, Jesus Christ himself being the chief Corner Stone. If this claim be well founded, whether they have a written history of one century or of twenty, matters little. Yet whatever of the past belongs to any, it may be well to know. And Baptist history constitutes one of the most interesting chapters in the records of Christianity.

During the apostolic age even, the doctrines of the gospel became corrupted, and its ordinances soon after. Both Jewish and Gentile converts brought into the churches many of their old religious notions, and incorporated them with the faith of Christ. These, together with the many philosophical ideas of the times and the perversions to which the truth is always exposed from the ignorance and selfishness of men, very early turned the churches aside from the faith once delivered to the saints. Still there were many who in simplicity and humility maintained the doctrines and customs in their original purity. Those churches which were strongest and most prosperous were most exposed to corruption by alliances with the world.

When at length the period of martyrdom and persecution terminated; when a nominal Christianity took possession of a throne, and Church and State became united, then religion, in its prevailing forms, lost its simplicity, its spirituality, and its power, and a temporal hierarchy took the place of the church of Christ. This was the great apostasy of the early times. But all the churches and all disciples did not follow in the wake of this sad departure from the truth. Many congregations and communities of true worshipers kept the doctrines of the gospel, and practiced its ordinances, nearly, or quite, in their primitive purity. And this they continued to do through all the ages of darkness and corruption which followed. They were never identified with the Roman or Greek churches; they never were in alliance with States; never formed hierarchies. As independent congregations, or small communities, with no other bond of union than a common faith, fellowship, and sympathy, often obscure and unobtrusive, taking the word of God as their guide, they sought to realize the idea, not of a temporal, but a spiritual kingdom in the gospel dispensation.

These religious communities were by the dominant hierarchies called *sects*, and stigmatized as *heretics*. As such they were traduced and persecuted continually. And though they may have had their errors, they were the best and purest defenders of the Christian faith, and the truest representatives of the first disciples of Christ then existing. The State churches were the heretics; while those so-called sects were the true successors of the first Christians.

They were defamed and oppressed. Calumniated and martyred because they bore witness to the truth of God and testified against the errors and vices of the so-called churches. History has never done them justice, and perhaps never will; because history has been too much written in the interest of their enemies, or from their standpoint. Tortured and tormented by those who should have been their defenders, crowns and mitres alike pledged to their destruction, they could do nothing but suffer. And this they nobly did as Christ's faithful witnesses. They were known by various names in different ages and in different lands, but retained the same general characteristics.

In the *first* and *second* centuries, Messalians, Montanists, Euchites, were terms which distinguished some of these sects.

In the *third, fourth* and *fifth* centuries arose the Novatians. Increasing with exceeding rapidity, they quite overspread the

Roman empire, in spite of the cruel and destructive persecutions which they suffered.

In the *fourth* century the Donatists appeared, as a new form of existing sects, or a new phase of the old faith. They multiplied rapidly, spread extensively, and long survived.

In the *seventh* century appeared the Paulicians, attracting much attention, and calling down upon themselves the wrath of the Romish Church. Still they increased greatly, notwithstanding their many persecutions.

That these Christian communities should have been faultless could not be supposed. But they were the best of the ages in which they lived, and maintained the purest forms of gospel truth and practice. Without the advantage of organization and association, they differed somewhat among themselves.

But in general they all professed to take the New Testament as the rule of their faith and practice. They held to a spiritual church membership, and received only professedly regenerated persons to the ordinances. Denying the orthodoxy of the Romish Church, they re-baptized persons received from that body, and hence were called *Anabaptists.* Infant baptism they rejected, according to Allix, Mosheim, Robinson, and other historians. Baptism they administered by immersion, as indeed did all Christians during those ages. Robinson calls them "Trinitarian Baptists." It is said that the Empress Theodora, after having confiscated their property, caused to be cruelly put to death no less than one hundred thousand Paulicians, for no other fault or offense than their religious faith.

.About the close of the *tenth* century appeared the Paterines;. substantially the same people, no doubt, as had previously existed under other names. They too rejected infant baptism, and protested against the corruptions of the Romish Church; in consequence of which they suffered long and severe persecutions.

In the *eleventh* century, and the ages following, were the Waldenses, Albigenses, Vaudois, Cathari, and Poor Men of Lyons. These were new names, and names usually given by their enemies. They increased, even under their persecutions, to a wonderful extent, and attracted the notice, if not the sympathy, of all Europe.

It is not pretended that these ancient

sects were known by name as Baptists; but in general they held the more prominent and distinctive principles which have always characterized the Baptists; thus: 1. They declared and defended the rights of faith and conscience and the freedom of worship. 2. They denied the authority of popes and the right of kings and States to interfere with the people in matters of religion. 3. They rejected infant baptism. 4. They baptized by dipping. 5. They held the Bible to be the only rule and authority in concerns of religious faith and practice. 6. They admitted none to the churches except such as professed to be regenerated and godly persons.

Now it is conceded by all historians of note that such churches and communities did exist, separate from and persecuted by, the prevailing State churches and civil authorities during all the ages from the Apostles to the Reformation.

When the Reformation under Luther and his coadjutors broke out, these sects to a great extent fraternized with, and were lost in the multitude of the reformers. Such as continued their separate existence, as the Waldenses of Piedmont, yielding to the influence of the reformers, did from sympathy what the persecutions of the Papists had never been able to compel them to do—abandon dipping for sprinkling in baptism, adopted infant baptism, and took the general forms of religious life, into which Pedobaptist Protestantism grew.

THE WELSH BAPTISTS.

Few denominations have a better claim to antiquity than the Welsh Baptists. They trace their descent directly from the Apostles, and urge in favor of their claim arguments which have never been confuted.

When Austin, the Romish monk and missionary, visited Wales, at the close of the *sixth* century, he found a community of more than two thousand Christians, quietly living in their mountain homes. They were independent of the Romish See, and wholly rejected its authority. Austin labored hard to convert them—that is, to bring them under the Papal yoke; but entirely failed in the effort. Yielding things in general, he reduced his demand upon them to three particulars. 1. That they should observe Easter in due form, as ordered by the church. 2. That they should give Christendom, or baptism, to their children. 3. That they should preach to the English the word of God, as directed.[1]

These demands of Austin prove that they neither observed the Popish ordinance of Easter, nor baptized their children. They however rejected all his overtures, whereupon he left them with threats of war and wretchedness. Not long after, Wales was invaded by the Saxons, and many of these inoffensive Christians cruelly murdered, as was believed, at the instigation of this bigoted zealot, the exacting Austin.

THE DUTCH BAPTISTS.

The Baptists of Holland have a history that reaches back to a very remote period, if not to the apostolic age, as some confidently assert. And this antiquity is conceded by historians who have no sympathy with their denominational sentiments.

MOSHEIM, in his church history, says: "The true origin of that sect which acquired the name Anabaptist *is hid in the remote depths of antiquity*, and is consequently extremely difficult to be ascer-

[1] See Benedicts Hist. Bap., p. 343, and authorities there cited.

tained." *Eccl. Hist. Vol. IV., p. 427. Mac. Ed., 1811.* See *Introd. Orchard's Hist. Bap., p. 17.*

ZWINGLE, the Swiss reformer, contemporary with Luther, declares: "The institu- of Anabaptism is no novelty, but for *thirteen hundred years* has caused great disturbance in the church." *Introd. Orchard's Hist. Bap., p. 17.* Thirteen hundred years before his time would have carried it back to within two centuries of the death of Christ.

DR. DERMONT, chaplain to the king of Holland, and Dr. Ypeij, professor of theology at Groningen, a few years since received a royal commission to prepare a history of the Reformed Dutch Church. That history, prepared under royal sanction, and officially published, contains the following manly and generous testimony to the antiquity and orthodoxy of the Dutch Baptists. "We have now seen that the Baptists, who were formerly called Anabaptists, and in later times Mennonites, were the original Waldenses, and have long in the history of the church received the honor of that origin. On this account, *the Baptists may be considered the only Christian community which has stood since the apostles, and as a Christian society, which has preserved pure the doctrines of the gospel through all ages." Hist. Ref. Dutch Ch., Ed. Breda, 1819.* See *Ency. Relig. Knowledge, Art. Mennonites.*

MOSHEIM says of the persecutions of this people in the sixteenth century: "Vast numbers of these people, in nearly all the countries of Europe, would rather perish miserably by drowning, hanging, burning, or decapitation, than renounce the opinions they had embraced." And their innocency he vindicates thus: "It is indeed true that many Anabaptists were put to death, not as being bad citizens, or injurious members of civil society, but as being incurable *heretics*, who were condemned by the old canon laws. For the error of *adult baptism* was in that age looked upon as a horrible offence." That was their only crime. *Eccl. Hist., Cent. 16, Sec. 3, part 2, Ch. III. Fuller's Ch. Hist., B. 4.*

This testimony is all the more welcome, because it comes from those who have no ecclesiastical sympathies with Baptists, but who, in fidelity to history, bear honest testimony to the truth which history teaches.

The circumstances under which their evidence was produced give it additional force.

CARDINAL HOSSIUS, chairman of the council at Trent, says: "If the truth of religion were to be judged of by the readiness and cheerfulness which a man of any sect shows in suffering, then the opinions and persuasions of no sect can be truer or surer, than those of the *Anabaptists;* since there have been none, for these *twelve hundred years past*, that have been more grievously punished." *Orchard's Hist. Bap., Sec. 12, part 30, p. 364.*

Many thousands of the Dutch Baptists, called Anabaptists, and Mennonists, miserably perished by the hands of their cruel persecutors, for no crime but their refusal to conform to established churches.[1]

THE ENGLISH BAPTISTS.

At what time the Baptists appeared in England in definite denominational form, it is impossible to say. But from the *twelfth* to the *seventeenth* century, many of them

---

[1] Benedict's Hist. Baptists, Ch. IV. Neal's Hist. Puritans, Vol. II., p. 355. Supplement Fuller's Ch. Hist., B. 4.

suffered cruel persecutions, and death by burning, drowning, and beheading, besides many other, and sometimes most inhuman tortures. And this they suffered both from Papists and Protestants, condemned by both civil and ecclesiastical tribunals, only because they persisted in worshiping God according to the dictates of their consciences, and because they would not submit their religious faith and worship to the dictates of popes and princes.[1] In 1538, royal edicts were issued against them, and several were burnt at the stake in Smithfield.

BRANDE writes that: "In the year 1538, thirty-one Baptists, that fled from England, were put to death at Delft, in Holland; the men were beheaded, and the women were drowned." *Hist. Reformers.* See *Benedict's Hist. Bap., p. 303. Neal's Hist. Puritans, Vol. I., p. 138. Note, Vol. II., p. 355, Sup.* What crime had they committed to merit such treatment as this?

BISHOP LATIMER declares that: "The Baptists that were burnt in different parts of the kingdom went to death intrepidly, and without any fear, during the time of Henry

---

[1] See Histories of Baptists, by Crosby, Ivimey, Danvers, and Benedict.

VIII." *Lent Sermons. Neal's Hist. Purit., Vol. II., p. 356.*

Under the rule of the Popish Mary, they suffered perhaps no more than under that of the Protestant Elizabeth. During the reign of the latter a congregation of Baptists was discovered in London, whereupon several were banished, twenty-seven imprisoned, and two burnt at Smithfield.[1]

DR. FEATLEY, one of their bitter enemies, wrote of them, in 1633: "This sect, among others, hath so far presumed upon the patience of the State, that it hath held weekly conventicles, rebaptizing hundreds of men and women together in the twilight, in rivulets, and in some arms of the Thames, and elsewhere, dipping them all over head and ears. It hath printed divers pamphlets in defence of their heresy; yea, and challenged some of our preachers to disputation." *Eng. Bapt. Jubilee Memor., Benedict's Hist. Bapt., p. 304.*

BAILEY wrote, in 1639, that: "Under the shadow of independency they have lifted up their heads, and increased their numbers above all sects in the land. They have

---

[1] Wall, cited by Neal, Hist. Puritans, Vol. I., p. 137. Vol. II., p. 358, Supplement.

forty-six churches in and about London. They are a people very fond of religious liberty, and very unwilling to be brought under bondage of the judgment of others." *Benedict's History, p. 304.*

The first book published in the English language on the subject of baptism was translated from the Dutch, and bears date 1618. From this time they multiplied rapidly through all parts of the kingdom. The first regularly organized church among them, known as such in England, dates from 1607, and was formed in London by a Mr. Smyth, previously a clergyman of the established church.

In 1689, the Particular Baptists, so called, held a convention in London, in which more than one hundred congregations were represented, and which issued a confession of faith, still in use and highly esteemed.

The last Baptist martyr in England was Edward Wightman, of Burton upon Trent, condemned by the Bishop of Coventry, and burnt at Litchfield, April 11, 1612.[1]

AMERICAN BAPTISTS.

The history of American Baptists runs

[1] Eng. Bap. Jubilee Memor., Benedict's Hist. Bap.

back a little more than two and a quarter centuries. In this country, as elsewhere, they were cradled amidst persecution, and nurtured by the hatred of their foes. This has been their fortune in every age, and in every land.

ROGER WILLIAMS, a distinguished and an honored name, was identified with the rise of the denomination in America. He has been called their founder, because he organized the first church, and was intimately connected with their early history. Williams was born in Wales, 1598, educated at Oxford, England, came to America in 1630, and settled as minister of the Puritan church in Salem, Massachusetts. Not long after he adopted Baptist views of doctrine and church order, on account of which he was banished by his fellow Puritans, and driven out of Massachusetts, in the depths of a rigorous winter, in a new and inhospitable country. Having wandered far and suffered much, finding the savage Indians more generous and hospitable than his fellow Christians, he finally reached and fixed his future home at what is now Providence, R. I. Here, with a few associates of like faith, he founded a new colony, calling both the city and the colony *Providence,* in recognition of the divine guidance and protection, which he had in so remarkable a manner experienced.

In 1639, Mr. Williams received baptism from one of his associates, there being no minister to perform that service. He in turn baptized his associates, and a church was organized, of which he was chosen pastor. He was also appointed first Governor of Rhode Island. Full liberty was granted in matters of religion. Thus Roger Williams became the first ruler, and Rhode Island the first State which ever gave entire freedom to all persons to worship God, according to their own choice, without dictation or interference from civil or ecclesiastical authorities.

On account of this unrestricted liberty many Baptists, as well as other persecuted religionists from other colonies, and from Europe, collected in considerable numbers at Providence, and spread through the colony.

It is a mistake to suppose that all the Baptist churches in America grew out of the one which Roger Williams founded. It is even doubtful whether any single church arose as an outgrowth of that. As immigration increased, other churches grew up, having no connection with that; and with considerable rapidity the sentiments of Baptists spread into adjoining colonies, particularly west and south. For a long time, however, they were sorely persecuted, especially in Massachusetts and Connecticut. Persecuted even by those who had themselves fled from persecution in their native land, to find freedom and refuge in these distant wilds.

In 1644, the present First Church in Newport, R. I., was organized. But whether the present First Church in Providence was constituted before this date is still a disputed point. Both claim priority. In 1656, the Second Church, Newport, was formed. Then followed in order of time, the church in Swansea, Massachusetts, 1663; First, Boston, 1665; North Kingstone, R. I., 1665; Seventh Day Church, Newport, 1671; South Kingstone, R. I., 1680; Kittery, Me., 1682; Middletown, N. J., 1688; Lower Dublin, Pa., 1689; Charleston, S. C., 1690; Philadelphia, Pa., 1698; Welsh Tract, Del., 1701; Groton, Ct., 1705. Others, not mentioned, arose within this period in these and other Colonies. With the increase of population, Baptists rapidly increased and widely spread over the country.

Edward's Tables gives the number of American Baptist Churches in 1768, as only 137.

Asplund's Register for 1790, reported 872 churches, 722 ordained ministers, with 64,975 members.

Benedict's History states that in 1812, there were 2,633 churches, 2,143 ordained ministers, and 204,185 members.

Allen's Register for 1836, puts them at 7,299 churches, 4,075 ordained ministers, and 517,523 members.

The Baptist Year Book gives the following figures:

Date.	Churches.	Ministers.	Members.
1840	7,771	5,208	571,291
1860	12,279	7,773	1,016,134
1880	26,080	16,569	2,296,327
1890	33,588	21,175	3,070,047

The *Year Book* gives the Sunday-school statistics for 1890, as follows: For United States—Schools, 17,696; officers and teachers, 132,186; pupils, 1,211,698.

It must be borne in mind that the figures given in all these cases are less than the actual facts would warrant, since full reports from associations, churches, and schools can never be obtained.

OTHER BAPTISTS.

Besides the regular Baptist brotherhood, there are in the United States more than *a million* of other and smaller denominations, which practice *immersion*, but are not in fellowship with, nor reckoned as a part of the great Baptist family.

The Seventh Day Baptists, so-called on account of their observing Saturday, or the seventh day of the week, as their Sabbath, on the ground that the Jewish Sabbath was never abrogated. They are estimated at about 9,000.

The Free Will Baptists, who take their name from their views of the freedom of the human will. They practice open communion. Their number is about 114,700.

The Six Principle Baptists, thus designated because their doctrinal confession is based on the six points mentioned in Heb. 6 : 1, 2. Estimated at 1,450.

The Anti-Mission Baptists, called also Old Baptists, and Ironsides; found chiefly in the southwest. They do not favor missions, Sunday-schools, or other religious or moral reform movements, lest they should seem to interfere with the divine decrees. They are Antinomian in doctrine, and are said to number 45,000.

The Campbellites, Disciples, Reformers, or Christians, as they are variously called, estimated at 850,000.

The Winebrennorians, or Church of God. Estimated at about 30,000.

The Tunkers, or Dunkards, at 100,000 ; and the United Brethren at 200,000.

BAPTISTS ELSEWHERE.

In North America, aside from the United States, but including Canada, New Brunswick, Nova Scotia, Jamaica, and Cuba, about 140,000.

In Europe, including England, Scotland, Wales, Germany, and Sweden, about 405,000.

In Asia, including Burmah, and India, about 76,000.

In Australia, about 15,000.

In Africa, about 3,000.

THE END.

8 888007 122206